The Journal of Thomas H. Miller
Signalman Second Class
United States Navy
1943-1945

By
Thomas H. Miller and Lois Miller Latimer

Order this book online at www.trafford.com
or email orders@trafford.com

Most Trafford titles are also available at major online book retailers.

Printed in the United States of America.

ISBN: 978-1-4120-4879-8 (sc)
ISBN: 978-1-4907-5388-1 (e)

Trafford rev. 01/09/2015

www.trafford.com

North America & international
toll-free: 1 888 232 4444 (USA & Canada)
fax: 812 355 4082

The Journal of T.H. Miller

This book is the memoirs of
Thomas H. Miller researched
and written in journal form.

Friday, February 12, 1943

I enlisted in the U.S. Navy eight months ago. I've been on leave since that time, awaiting my forty-eight hour notice. Today I got my letter. The induction notice reads as follows: Thomas Miller please report to 29 Plymouth Court, Chicago, Illinois on Monday, February 15, at 8 a.m. to be inducted into the U.S. Navy.

I voluntarily joined the navy. I knew, eventually, serving would be inevitable and I didn't want to be in the army or the marines. Now I'm wondering if volunteering was such a good idea.

Monday, February 15, 1943

I reported to 29 Plymouth Court, only to be told to return tomorrow. I hope this isn't an indication of things to come.

Tuesday, February 16, 1943

At 8 o'clock this morning I was inducted into the U.S. Navy. There wasn't much of a ceremony. I don't know what I was expecting, but I guess I thought there would be more to it. About two hundred of us stood and said the oath in unison, then signed some papers and that was it.

I'm seeing guys from all walks of life. We are all from Chicago, but I never met them before. I guess we'll be together in very different circumstances. Some of us will probably face situations we never thought possible.

Friday, February 19, 1943

At 7:45 a.m., after three days of official leave, I boarded a train at Union Station bound for Farragut, Idaho and the U.S. Naval Training Station. There was no one to see me off. I said good-bye to my mom and sister at home. At the station the platform was crowded with people sending off their sons and sweethearts. It's a common scene these days, but I preferred to set off by myself.

The atmosphere on board is very light. There's a lot of joking and laughing. I'm learning to play cribbage. It's not complicated, but I'll probably forget it when this is all over.

The food's not bad. We didn't have fish for supper tonight because there was none available, but the officer said all religious leaders agreed that it was alright for Catholics to eat meat even though it was Friday.

Saturday, February 20, 1943

I awoke this morning to find out we were only as far as Cedar Rapids, Iowa. The train ride is slow and monotonous. Every couple of hours we pull off on a side track and allow other trains to pass. I guess this is what it means to get "side-tracked".

Sunday, February 21, 1943

Our train has just stopped for coal and water in North Platte, Nebraska. We were allowed to get off the train for awhile. The people of North Platte had set up welcome tables and were serving coffee, cakes, cookies, and sandwiches. They were so friendly and welcoming. I spoke to one woman. She said they meet every train that comes through town from 5 a.m. to midnight. With one or two trains every hour that adds up to 1500 to 2000 men everyday. Amazing!

10 p.m.

We crossed the Nebraska state line and entered Wyoming. We average about two states a day. The stops don't seem as frequent in this part of the country. Maybe we'll make better time, although I have no idea why I'm in such a hurry to get to get there.

Monday, February 22, 1943

We arrived at Camp Farragut at around three o'clock this morning. From the train station we had a ten mile bus ride to our barracks. This, we soon found out, was a disaster.

It seems the camp is still under construction and no where near completion. There are toilets and bunks, but only half the bunks have springs. There aren't even any mattresses. I was lucky enough to grab a bunk with a spring. Needless to say I didn't get the best nights sleep.

Anyway, there were about 1100 men on that troop train. Just imagine1100 tired men arriving to such a mess. I'll tell you what, chaos reigned supreme. There was almost a revolt. They threatened to call the shore patrol (the military police) if we didn't calm down. I'm not sure how, but eventually things quieted down. Maybe everyone was just too tired to fight.

At 6 a.m., after a few short hours of restless sleep, we assembled for roll call in what was supposed to be ranks. Our chief boatswain mate, named "Whip" McCord, is in charge of getting new recruits settled in. His favorite admonishment is, "Stop your crying! You're in the navy now! We'll make men of you, even if it kills you." Now, I hadn't been to the bathroom in about twenty-four hours and by this time I was in a bad way. When I got the chief's attention I made known my urgent need. His reply to my problem was, "Stay in ranks and shut up."

After roll call we marched to the mess hall for breakfast. As I said, the camp was no where near completion and there was only one mess hall to feed 12,000 men. We had to wait in chow line for an hour. I hadn't eaten since yesterday, but I ate very little breakfast. For the moment the need to relieve myself was stronger than my need to eat. As I emptied my tray in the trash barrel I asked the mess cook where the bathroom was. He answered, "The heads are on the other side of the grinder." *What*? I must have had a stupid look on my face, because he laughed at me. "The head," he said, "is the bathroom and the grinder is the drill field. The bathrooms are across the drill field by the barracks." I left him still laughing at me. The barracks were a half mile away. I knew I'd never make it. Once outside I looked around for a place to get the job done. I noticed a secluded place behind the mess hall where a dozen or more trash barrels were kept. No one was around, so I ran over behind the barrels. Suddenly, I heard this yell/bellow/roar, the likes of which I've never heard before. I'm discovered in this deplorable situation by, none other than, Chief McCord. His face turned livid red and looked as though it might explode. What did explode was a tirade of loud invective that would shame even a sailor. He took my name and promised I would be swabbing the deck of every barracks in the camp. As I write this, thinking about the incident makes me sick to my stomach. I'm tired, I'm hungry, and now Chief McCord is out to get me. I wish I was home.

Tuesday, February 23, 1943

We were issued our uniforms this morning. It's funny the store personnel never even measured me. They just glanced at me and immediately knew my shirt, shoe, and waist size. I weigh about 140 pounds, but most people would probably think I'm closer to 200. I thought these will never fit me, but they did.

After receiving our uniforms, dress and undress, we received our supplies. I'll list a few: duffel bag, blanket, mattress cover and (hallelujah) a mattress, pillow cover, pillow, towels, toilet articles, tooth brush, hair brush, sewing kit, scrub brush, whisk broom, jackknife, cap, drawers, gloves, handkerchiefs, neckerchiefs, dungarees, chambrays and flannel shirts, medium and heavy weight undershirts, cotton and woolen socks, overcoat, overshoes, raincoat, gym shoes. All these supplies, and more, have to be packed just so in our duffel bag, all packed according to navy regulation.

In the afternoon we were immunized for tetanus, malaria, small pox, and yellow fever. Everyone waited in line as a corpsman, with a tray of syringes, jabbed a needle into the arm in front of him, then the line moves on. If one does not move along fast enough he'll get jabbed again with another needle. It was all done in a rather rhythmic fashion.

I have to say I'm getting sick and tired of waiting in lines.

Wednesday, February 24, 1943

I've heard nothing from Chief McCord in regards to the incident which took place behind the mess hall. I'm always on the lookout for him, ready to dodge out of sight if I see him.

Friday, March 5, 1943

We are in quarantine. One of the guys in our company has scarlet fever. They say we will be in quarantine for the duration of our boot camp training. All this means is that we continue our training, but we'll receive no leave. No leave for fifteen weeks. This is unbearable. Boot camp is miserable. I've yet to see Chief McCord. It's been over a week. Maybe he's afraid of scarlet fever.

Monday, March 22, 1943

We've settled into a routine. We begin on the drill field, marching and doing calisthenics: 100 push-ups, 100 squat-thrusts, and 25 chin-ups. Our company commander R.J. Dobell is relentless on the drill field. We have to run around the three mile grinder, two to three times, depending on his mood. Another drill we often do involves pushing a twelve foot medicine ball to the end of the grinder. Two teams push against this huge ball, pushing it toward their end of the field. I hate it. I'm always getting stepped on or fallen upon.

In the afternoon we learn about navy tradition and routine, such as seamanship, navy rigging, and the different parts of a sailing barge. I've also learned to tie about a thousand different kinds of knots.

Again, in the evening we march and do calisthenics, after which we return to the barracks where I study "The Bluejacket's Manual" until about 9 o'clock. After that I write letters or write in this journal until the bugle plays taps and then it's lights out.

Wednesday, March 24, 1943

Very bad day! You have no idea what it's like to spend the day on the drill field in the pouring rain. Miserable!!! Today we did the "commando course". This is a mile long obstacle course with fifteen foot walls to scale, a huge rocky terrain to climb, and deep trenches to cross. The course had to be completed in a certain amount of time. I don't even know what the time requirement is. I don't care. All I know is that I made it. After this we had to do push-ups, chin-ups, and sit-ups until we absolutely could do no more. The purpose of this "strength test" is to see how physically fit we are. This grueling and exhausting exercise will be repeated again at the end of our training.

Friday, April 2, 1943

The navy has its own terminology for everything. I learned that early on. Most recently I've been learning the terminology for parts of a ship. For example, the bow is the front, or forward end of the ship. The stern is the back, or aft end. Starboard is on the right hand side looking forward and port side is on the left side looking forward. It's a language all its own. With words like sternpost, bilge keels, cut water, scuppers, stanchions, and tiller. It's a language I one day hope to be fluent in.

Monday, April 5, 1943

Payday! We get paid the fifth and twentieth of every month. As an apprentice seaman I receive $15 every payday, $30 a month. I'll leave it in my account to accumulate and draw cash out as I need it. I don't need much cash. Anything I need from the camp store is purchased then deducted from my account.

The Journal of T.H. Miller

Wednesday, April 14, 1943

An incredible thing happened today. While leaving the mess hall after breakfast, I found myself face to face with Chief McCord. I didn't even have a chance to duck out of sight. He returned my salute without even a glimmer of recognition. I do believe he's forgotten the entire incident. I hope so.

Thursday, April 22, 1943

With great interest I've been learning and studying about our naval fleet. It is without a doubt the most formidable and powerful military entity. The fleet is comprised of about fifty ships: aircraft carriers, battleships, cruisers, and destroyers. The fleet is broken down into three task forces. These task forces may be separated by hundreds of miles. Each task force is further broken down into three to four task groups. Task groups are the smallest unit and are positioned together. It's made up of fifteen to twenty ships. Two to three aircraft carriers are in the center of the formation, because they are the most valuable. They are floating air bases and are the target of enemy attacks. Flanking the carriers are two to three cruisers and one to two battleships. They act as anti-aircraft defense. On the outside, in the most vulnerable position, are ten to twelve destroyers. They act as the anti-submarine screen. The destroyer is an all around fighting ship and the most versatile. They are fast, maneuverable, and have tremendous fire power, but they have two disadvantages. First, they don't carry enough fuel to stay with the other ships very long and must be refueled from the diesel tanks of other ships. Second, they must get close to an enemy ship to fire upon it. The risk in this is obvious. The cruisers, the battleships, and the destroyers have just one task and that is to protect the aircraft carriers.

Monday, May 3, 1943

An incident happened today that shows just how ridiculous boot camp can be. It seems someone yelled an obscene remark at Dobell. As no one would say who said it, the entire company was required to walk/run laps around the grinder until the guilty party confessed. This continued for six hours. I never found out who it was.

Monday, May 17, 1943

All week we've been sailing on a glacial lake called Coeur D' Alene Lake, learning what is called "marlinespike seamanship". This deals with rope and the methods of working with it, using knotting, splicing, and seizing. We call it "handling lines".

There were fifteen of us manning the small sail boat, called a sloop. This can be a hazardous undertaking. It takes team work and timing to handle the ropes and steer with the tiller. It was going well until today when our boat capsized. We ended up in the ice cold water. Luckily a motor launch, which was patrolling in case we ran into trouble, picked us up shortly after we capsized. We were wearing lifejackets so there was no danger of our drowning, but we wouldn't have lasted long in such frigid water. I will say the navy does everything to ensure our safety!! After that we were immediately sent back to the barracks to take hot showers.

Monday, May 31, 1943

Today we did our abandon ship drill. We jumped about twenty feet into a pool of water with a life jacket on. If this is not done correctly the arms can be pulled right out of their sockets. What you have to do is cross your arms over your chest and grab hold of your life jacket. Jumping from that height seems to take an eternity to hit the water.

Tuesday, June 8, 1943

Another requirement for boot camp is to swim seventy-five yards, which today I just barely accomplished. I have never been a very good swimmer. From time to time, while swimming, I would reach for the side of the pool. Walking right beside me was Dobell. Every time I reached for the edge he hit my arm with a life preserver and yelled, "There's not going to be anyone in my company who can't swim!"

Saturday, June 12, 1943

Throughout the past weeks there has been a lot of riding, horse play, and practical jokes. This kind of fun is what makes this place tolerable. One recruit, named John Bater, has been the brunt of many jokes. Apparently he's been trying to get a medical discharge. Although he looks healthy enough to me, he's always in sick bay and he takes a whole slew of pills. Anyway, last night after the bugle had played taps, all the lights were out, and everything was quiet, a voice suddenly cried out, "**Hey! Don't forget to give Bater his pill!!**" It was so funny! The whole barracks erupted into laughter. There was snickering even after twenty minutes. Writing about it now makes me want to laugh.

Sunday, June 13, 1943

I dread tomorrow. We have to run the commando course again. This time knowing what to expect only makes it worse.

Monday, June 14, 1943

It's over!! It wasn't any harder than the first time, but it certainly wasn't any easier. I'm just glad to be through it.

Thursday, June 17, 1943

I've heard rumors that Henry Fonda is supposed to be here at Camp Farragut. This is a huge camp with over ten thousand men, so seeing him would be purely by chance. Well, chance would have it that I was able to get just a glimpse of him. This morning I saw him running with his company down the stairs from the barracks toward the drill field. Then he disappeared into the ranks. Those who have some contact with him say he keeps pretty much to himself.

Monday, June 21, 1943

Something happened today which I can add to my list of "life's most embarrassing moments". We were assembled in ranks for inspection by the commander of the base, Commander Gustifson. We were executing the manual of arms. At the command "present arms", I snapped my arm out straight and my rifle slipped out of my hand and rattled across the floor. Dobell immediately retrieved the rifle. He returned it to me and through clenched teeth said, "You're going to wear this around your neck for a week."

The Journal of T.H. Miller

Tuesday, June 22, 1943

I've finished boot camp. There was a short ceremony this afternoon where I was promoted to seaman 2nd class. It's been the toughest sixteen weeks of my life, but I'm proud of my accomplishment.

We've been granted three days liberty in Spokane, Washington, followed by a ten day leave to go home. Frankly, I'd rather skip Spokane and go directly home.

Friday, June 26, 1943

My three days in Spokane are coming to an end. It proved to be very disappointing. There is an army camp near Spokane and the town is crowded with servicemen. As you look down the street there is a sea of white hats and garrison caps. All of us wandering and looking for entertainment. There's no place to spend the night. All the hotels, boarding houses, and rental space are full. My buddy, Frank Rod, and I went around to the bars. There's not much else to do. We were able to find a place to sleep in the basement of a Lutheran church. They had mattresses spread out on the floor and in the morning they served coffee and cookies. My only solace is tomorrow I'll be on a train for home. The thought of going home, even for a few days, is a wonderful thing to look forward to.

Sunday, June 27, 1943

I'm on board a train heading home. Of the ten days, six will be spent enroute. Oh well, those are the breaks. I'll spend those four days, most likely, dreading the end when I have to return to Idaho.

This train is an old coach without much ventilation. Smoke and soot from the old coal burning engine fill this

14

cattle car I'm traveling in. It's not a very pleasant travel experience. I'm afraid I can only give this railroad line a one star rating.

Tuesday, June 29, 1943

Travel has been slow and monotonous. Again, we pull off on a side track every couple of hours to allow faster trains to pass. Within an hour, however, we should be pulling into Union Station. I can't describe the excitement I feel at being home again. I have such a short time to spend with family and friends. I must make the most of it.

Saturday, July 3, 1943

The past four days flew by like minutes. I would have liked to been able to slip away quietly when the time came to say goodbye. I hate good-byes, so I didn't allow anyone to come to the station with me. Saying goodbye to my family at home was bad enough. I didn't want to be a part of the real life melodrama that goes on everyday at the train station. I've never known loneliness like what I felt taking the L to Union Station. I don't think I'll ever forget that lonely, sick at heart feeling for as long as I live.

Just now thoughts of my survival are starting to overwhelm me. I'm having doubts as to whether I'll ever return. As reassurance I remind myself that my intuition is seldom accurate. This makes me feel somewhat better.

Monday, July 5, 1943

I arrived back at Farragut around 6 p.m.. I'm wondering what's next. Tomorrow we begin testing to determinc our talents and how they might be put to use to help win the war.

Payday! As seaman 2nd class, I'm now making $36.00 a month.

Thursday, July 8, 1943

The aptitude tests we took lasted three days. Some of us, it was determined, have leadership qualities. They are sent on to the V-12 program (officer's training). It has been decided that "yours truly" will make a good signalman. How they determined this I can't imagine.

Monday, July 12, 1943

Quartermaster-Signalman School, also known as service school, is much different than boot camp, thank goodness. It has been an awakening experience for me. I have great respect for our instructors. They are men who escaped death after their ships were torpedoed and sunk. They are strong, determined, conscientious, and brave. They are not commissioned officers, but petty officers. It's these men who are the back-bone of the navy. The ones who gallantly defend our country while at sea. They've been granted "shore duty", serving as instructors in the service school. They are all career men with at least two stripes. Each strip equals four years of service.

Wednesday, July 14, 1943

I've learned that Quartermaster School and Signalman School are two different studies. Quartermaster is strictly navigation, while the signalman studies communication. I understand I will receive some navigational instruction, but I will mainly be learning communication.

The Journal of T.H. Miller

Sunday, August 1, 1943

I've had very little time to keep this journal up to date. Service school requires a lot of studying and practicing. I need to be prepared because the most challenging test is yet to come, when I'm required to function independently as a full-fledged signalman. One has to be alert, quick, calm, and in control. Navy ships, particularly combat ships, operate in formation with other vessels. They perform complicated maneuvers in close proximity and at high speeds, operating under radio silence in fog, smoke, darkness, and frequently without lights. They depend entirely on visual communication. The duties of the signalman are indeed critical to the safe and efficient maneuvering of all ships. The signalman can be proud of their skills. No one among the ship's crew can do what they do, not even the captain. But these duties are hectic and stressful. Errors or negligence while on watch could result in catastrophic consequences. It's all very unnerving.

Saturday, August 27, 1943

I have had several instructors so far in service school. W.R. Morgan is the CMS (chief signalman), the others are A.T. Morgan, H.H. McCants, J.W. Knox, E.F. Fitzgerald, and V.J. Hutchinson.

Hutchinson, or Hutch as he's called, is a first class signalman. He's a survivor of the cruiser Vincennes, which sunk with two other ships in Guadalcanal Harbor. He has conducted the majority of our training. He's a tough task master and has no tolerance for mistakes that are the result of carelessness. If a student is careless or indifferent and an error is made in some procedure, he becomes outraged and severely scolds and lectures on how such carelessness would

17

cost lives and would only aid the enemy in their war effort. Quite honestly the weight of this responsibility seems almost too much to bear.

This is the eighth week of our training. It's hard to believe we're half way through. We continue to learn all there is to know about navy communication, while at the same time practicing and mastering what we've already learned. As I previously mentioned during war time there is radio silence. Therefore, the sole means of communication is by visual signals. This is what I've been learning for the past eight weeks. We communicate by several different means. First, is the flashing light which uses the Morse code system of dots and dashes. This is a twelve inch search light with a shutter that opens and closes by means of a spring loaded handle. In some cases a thirty-six inch carbon arch search light is used when great distances separate the ships. Another method of communication is called flag hoist. This uses alphabet flags, numeral flags, and various pennants. These flags are a coded system that is a language in itself. The messages are interpreted by an international signal book, which is agreed upon and used by all the countries of the world. Yet another form of communication is the semaphore signal system. This is when two hand flags are used. These flags are held at different positions for different letters. Messages are spelled out in this way. This means of communication must be done at close range. As I said there are several different means of communication these are just a few.

Friday, October 29, 1943
After sixteen weeks of Quartermaster-Signalman school, I have graduated and have been promoted to seaman

first class. I've also learned that upon graduating I earned two college credits for my training. Imagine that!! Maybe I'll consider going to college when this is all over.

Monday, November 1, 1943
Everyone from my class has received their assignment. They have been sent to various parts of the country, assigned to naval and merchant marine ships on both the east and west coast. Everyone has been assigned except "yours truly". Apparently, they have no place to send me.

Friday, November 5, 1943
Payday! As seaman first class, I now make $54 a month.

Monday, November 8, 1943
I spent the past week reading and studying in the barracks. It's easy to concentrate (but hard to stay awake) because the barracks are so quiet. I'm not alone. There are a few others who, like me, are left over: machinist mates, yeoman (office workers), electricians mates, boatswain mates (they maintain the hull of the ship and the small boats on board), and ordinance men (ammunition), but I'm the only signalman. I'm actually referred to as a signalman striker. This is like a signalman trainee. I'll be a striker until I achieve the rating of a petty-officer.

Monday, November 15, 1943
Today I received my assignment. I've been assigned, as a one-man draft, to the heavy cruiser U.S.S. Boston. The Boston is part of cruiser division ten, a three ship unit

comprising of the Boston, the Baltimore, and the Chicago. At this time the Boston is on her shakedown cruise (this is like a test cruise). I'm to go to San Francisco and wait for her to arrive at Alameda Naval Base. From there we go on active duty in the Pacific theater of war.

Tuesday, November 23, 1943
I am alone here in the barracks in San Francisco. Up until now I shared it with two other men named Frank Minicci and Leo O'Dwyer. They were waiting to be assigned to shore-duty after seeing action in the Solomon Islands. They have gone home to their families for Thanksgiving. After the holiday they'll be stationed in Norfolk. They spent most of their time here harassing me. I'm sure it was all meant in fun because when they left they wished me good luck and God speed. I miss their company and I'm feeling very lonely.

Thanksgiving Day, November 25, 1943
I decided to visit a U.S.O. center. They try, somehow, to cheer up servicemen away from home by providing entertainment. At some U.S.O. centers celebrities volunteer their time and talents. All and all, the shows are not too bad. Although there were no celebrities at the location I visited, they did have a good band that I enjoyed listening to. While I was there I struck up a conversation with a civilian who wanted to do his part for the war effort. He invited me to his home to share Thanksgiving dinner with his family. He was so kind. He offered to pick me up, but I declined. He gave me directions to his home. I'm ashamed to admit it, but I never showed up. I can't explain why. I had every intention of going, but feeling so depressed and lonely it's difficult to

arouse from this stupor. The effort is just too great. It's easier to be alone. Frankly, I don't think I would be very good company anyway. I know these are just lame excuses and there are no justifiable reasons for my behavior. So here I am back at the barracks writing this. I wonder what he will think when he realizes that the serviceman he invited to share Thanksgiving dinner with is not going to show up.

Tuesday, November 30, 1943

I'm finally going to board the Boston. It came into port last night upon completion of its shakedown cruise. Someone will be here in an hour to pick me up.

I have a strange feeling about the future. I guess I could call it apprehension. I can't even imagine what it's like to be in a war zone. I'm wondering when I'll see the U.S. again. I hope and pray I will survive. I'm sure every serviceman is praying the same prayer. I'll be philosophical about this and say, "What ever will be will be." I will not dwell on thoughts of dying. Truthfully, the thought of dying is not as troubling as the thought of my mother and what she would go through in the event of my death.

8 p.m.

I was picked up at the barracks at eight o'clock this morning. A first class seaman drove me to Alameda Naval Base in Oakland. We crossed the recently opened Oakland Bay Bridge, a ten mile long suspension bridge. It was so foggy this morning I saw little of the bridge or what surrounded it. My chauffeur proceeded to relate to me the great times he's had at the night spots of San Francisco and San Diego. The fact that I found California the most depressing place in the world I kept to myself. His opinion of the area in contrast to my impression made me feel I should have been classified 4-F (physically unfit for military service). He then continued to eloquently expound upon the merits of "sea-duty". He told me the best "sea-duty" could be compared to the worst "shore-duty". I have no idea what this means.

We arrived at Alameda and parked along the dock where the Boston was moored. When I first caught sight of the ship, I was awe-struck by the size of this great man-of-war, a massive steel structure of towers and turrets. The huge hull rose twenty feet above me to the main deck. Its length looked to be about four city blocks. This will be my new home. I wonder if its awesomeness will lessen with time.

Upon arriving at the ship my driver instructed me on the procedure for boarding and the protocol that must be observed. I guess it was part of his duty as recruiting and induction specialist. I was instructed to go up the gang plank, salute the flag, turn to the man on watch and request permission to come on board. Upon his command to "advance and be recognized", I stepped forward and submitted my orders. The man then summoned the officer of the watch who, after returning my salute, proceeded to peruse my four pages of type written orders. He questioned me about my service school training. "Who was my commanding officer?" I was even questioned about my home town of Chicago. "Where's the Chicago Stadium and what's its purpose?" I don't believe this officer was ever in Chicago. I suppose this was all part of the routine. I'm sure he didn't suspect me of being a spy. Following the interview I was told to report to the signal bridge. They were expecting me.

I was escorted to the signal bridge, on the forward super structure, where I was presented to the signal officer as the "one man draft" that completed the compliment of the Admiral's staff. It was explained to me that I was not a member of the ship's company, but one of the elite "flag" (the Admiral's staff). Apparently, the Admiral has his own staff which I'm apart of, along with yeoman, bos'n mates, coxswains, and machinists. As part of his staff I have to be available to him and, therefore, I'm exempt from ship's duties. I will be responsible for raising flag hoist and assisting rated personnel in the reading of the flashing light and spotting the command ship for the latest signals. I was immediately assigned a "dog" watch. There are two, two hour "dog" watches, from 4:00 to 6:00 p.m. and 6:00 to 8:00 p.m.. These watches accommodate the supper hour. All other watches are four hours long. We rotate through four hour on, eight hours off. My first watch is the 1800-2000 (6 p.m.-8 p.m.) "dog" watch. I was then dismissed to go below and stow my gear. I was told to report back to the bridge when we got underway.

I was assigned a locker and a bunk on the second deck below the main deck. The bunks are stacked four high with just enough room to walk between. Mine is the top most bunk. I can just barely turn over. There is only about 18 inches from my mattress to the "over-head".

At 1400 (2 p.m.) all hands were "piped" to report to stations to prepare to get underway. Aboard ship the bos'n pipe is used to alert all hands that an announcement is to follow over the intercom system. The bos'n pipe is a little whistle about six inches long. It makes a very shrill sound.

I immediately proceeded to the signal bridge. There I came upon, what appeared to be, complete pandemonium. Men were hurrying about, shouting, and jostling one another. I was not sure what I was supposed to do. No one even seemed to notice me. I stood back out of the way watching some men attach signal flags end to end and hoist them on a halliard (rope) up to the yardarm (cross bar) high upon the mast of the forward super structure. Out on the wing of the bridge men were operating the signal light.

I felt a vibration on the deck of the bridge and noticed the ship slowly moving. We were underway. Within minutes the landscape was quickly slipping by. The movement was so smooth. It was as if the objects were moving and not the ship. It was hard to imagine this giant dreadnought moving at all, let alone so swift and smoothly.

After about ten minutes the activity began to abate. Men moved to the rail of the bridge and looked toward the shore. I moved to a spot where I could see forward. The bow of the ship was cutting through the water of San Francisco Bay. I felt a slight roll as the bow dipped. I felt the mist on my face. The Golden Gate Bridge was slowly coming toward us. I was transfixed. The rolls of the ship were becoming more pronounced. The bow plunges into a giant swell and sent up a huge spray of water. I began to notice another sensation, an uneasiness in my stomach. I was becoming seasick.

At this point a big, tall guy with blond hair and a toothy grin approached me and offered his hand. "You must be the new man," he said. He introduced himself as Bill Anderson, second class signalman. He seemed very likable. I've been assigned to his watch. Feeling lousy I request permission to go below. I stayed in my bunk until supper for the watch was "piped". The first to be called are the mess cooks, the steward mates, and the officers. The cooks and steward mates eat first because they prepare and serve the food. The officers eat first because…they're officers. Next in line to eat are the ship's company and then the watch. I waited and listened. Finally, I heard "supper for the second watch".

Enlisted men are served by going through the "chow" line. The line moves fast. I was served and seated in about twenty minutes. Meals are served for one hour. In that time one can go through as often as he pleases. I guess this is where the term "chow hound" comes from.

While waiting in line something so disturbing happened, I've been able to think of little else. A man up ahead of me collapsed and died, from a massive heart attack I've since learned. It was amazing how fast the medical corpsmen were on the scene. The man was immediately wrapped in a black tarpaulin and removed. I've never seen someone die, much less right in front of me. This caused a whole new spectrum of thought to cross my mind. Does this represent something ominous and foreboding in my future? Why should I be present? I cursed the war and everything else that caused me to be present at this time and place in my life. I wish I was back home in Chicago.

I don't think I ate anything. I was sick and upset. I picked at my food and pushed it around my tray. It seemed like a long time before I heard the bos'n whistle and the announcement to, "relieve the watch". *Well, this is it,* I thought. I proceeded to the bridge to begin my first watch.

Anderson, who I had met earlier, greeted me most amicably. I told him what had happened in the chow-line, but he'd already heard about it. "You never know when your time is up," he said philosophically. To which I'd have to agree. I also told him I was seasick. He recommended I still keep eating. He went to the signal shack, which is a closet about four feet square and holds the coffee pot, forms, papers, and the logs. He returned with some saltines and gave them to me. I nibbled on them and it seemed to help. Anderson explained that feeling seasick was normal and should pass once we're out at sea. Being close to land the ocean swells are bigger and this causes the ship to roll and pitch. I found this encouraging. We stood on the lee side of the bridge (the side that's out of the wind) and talked about trivial things: where we were from, how things were back in the States. I learned he is a survivor from the cruiser North Hampton, which was torpedoed and sunk during the Coral Sea campaign.

At eight o'clock our watch was relieved and I went below deck. So ends my first day aboard the Boston. My attitude is improving. My first watch went well and my seasickness is much better. For awhile I laid on my bunk contemplating my situation. A year ago I never dreamed I'd find myself on ship headed for Pearl Harbor. I have no idea where I'll find myself a year from now. God willing, I'll still be alive. I tried to sleep before my next watch at 0400, but there is too much activity. So I've been updating my journal, which by the way is against regulation. Keeping a journal is considered a security risk. It may be confiscated, but I'm not too concerned about it. No one pays much attention to what I'm doing way up here on the top bunk. Also stated in "The Bluejackets Manual", gambling is strictly forbidden. I think I'll end here and see if I can get into that game of craps going on a few bunks down.

Wednesday, December 1, 1943

I'm afraid I'm off to a bad start with the chief signalman. His name is Chief Zook. His physical description could be out of a story book. He is short and fat with fire red hair and a personality to match. Although I've done nothing, I have the unmistakable feeling he does not like me. He informed me that the Admiral, Rear Admiral Wiltse, decided his people were subject to the same rules, regulations, and duties as the ship's crew. Chief Zook told me this with a gleam in his eye. This did not bother me in the least. In fact, I felt uneasy being exempt from certain duties and sensed some were reluctant to assign me to a task. With this change of events, Chief Zook proceeded to assign me to all the menial, tedious, and humbling duties he could think of. All the while riding and belittling me in everything I do. The only good thing is that Chief Zook is not required to stand watch at night. At night I'm spared his harassment.

In all fairness I must concede he is a good sailor and an ambitious one. He's also a survivor of the light cruiser Juneau which sank during the Solomon Islands campaign.

Thursday, December 2, 1943

We continue on our way to Pearl Harbor under condition three (non-emergency). We are sailing alone. On the first day we were escorted by a navy blimp, supposedly as an anti-submarine device. Now we are alone. I wonder about this. A new ship is an easy target for an enemy submarine. Cruisers are not equipped with sonar gear. We are literally a sitting duck. Now that we are on our own we have reduced our speed and are proceeding on a zigzag course. Zigzag courses are an important tactic in naval operations. If we happen to be spotted by an enemy aircraft scout our destination would be impossible to determine. There are many zigzag plans utilized during naval operations. Different plans are implemented every couple of hours.

There is very little activity on the bridge. The C.S. (communication signal) division comprises of about twenty men: first, second, and third class signalmen (three each), the chief signalman, and two signal officers (lieutenants). The rest are signalmen strikers (like me). During daylight operations there are as many as fifteen men on the bridge, after sunset only four men are needed. The ship is completely blacked out and out of necessity all visual communication must cease, but a watchful vigil is still maintained. Any strange object in the ocean must be identified. Each watch is under a supervisor. The supervisor is either the chief signalman, one of the signal officers, or a second or third class petty officer. The supervisor oversees the men of his watch and makes sure everyone is alert. He will also assist in flag hoist and reading the flashing light when it is busy.

I stand my watches, four hours on, eight hours off. The hours off are ours to do as we please. I am trying to make the most of it and enjoy the trip. The ship has a good library. I spend a lot of my time there reading. I prefer the classics: Dickens, Poe, Stevenson, and Thoreau. In my free time I also write letters and keep this journal up to date. Sometimes I play cards or checkers, but not very often. I don't feel much camaraderie with the other men on board. I don't know why. I hope this will change. Anderson, he's okay though. I spend a lot of time talking to him. The other enlisted men in the "flag" are second class signalman Ed Zimmerman and third class quartermaster Bill Jackson. Zimmerman is hard to get to know. He keeps to himself and doesn't say much. I find myself avoiding Jackson. He's kind of a sissy and I suspect not very well liked. He always wants to read his wife's letters to me and he spares no details. Of the signal officers, Lieutenant Nichols is pretty likable, but he doesn't show himself very often. Lieutenant Schwartz is a regular snob of an officer. I don't care much for him at all. My relationship with Chief Zook is about the same. However, in a rare departure, after learning I'm a musician, we had a good conversation about big bands. He's interested in big bands and popular music. I guess despite everything we do have a little in common.

While on watch we do flag hoist drills for expediency and accuracy. The signal originates on the port side and is decoded by the starboard. These exercises will ensure preparedness and efficiency when we join the fleet in Pearl Harbor. Also while on watch we keep a crucial log of what transpires while in port and underway. This is an accurate record of every incident that occurs. To be included in the log is the exact time and date, flag hoist signal, flashing light signal, and all message received and sent.

Friday, December 3, 1943

This being my first voyage at sea I am amazed at the number of flying fish I see. Huge droves of them, literally thousands at a time, fly into the path of the ship. Half go back into the water, the other half go over the ship. I found two or three dead ones on the deck. They are about eighteen inches long with huge fins or gills that act as wings. They are able to fly some distance, four to five hundred feet. It is such a strange sight.

Another strange thing about being at sea is one loses his sense of direction. Occasionally I check the gyro compass to get some idea of our direction.

The Journal of T.H. Miller

Saturday, December 4, 1943

An unbelievable thing happened today, unbelievably ridiculous. The ship stopped dead in the water. All hands were required to swim two laps around the ship. I couldn't believe it. I mean, these are shark infested waters. Although two launches with marine sharp shooters were detailed to patrol and watch for sharks, the whole business was down right dangerous. Not being the best swimmer, I didn't go far from the lower gang-way. They couldn't keep an eye on everyone, so no one noticed I wasn't doing much swimming. After about an hour or so we all came back on board and were underway again. Unbelievable, but true.

Sunday, December 5, 1943

We arrived at Pearl Harbor this morning. I was astounded at what I saw. It's been two years since the attack, but the devastation is still blatantly evident. The Arizona is still in the position it was following the attack with her mast tilted and her hull submerged. The entire harbor is covered with two inches of diesel oil. I can't imagine how long it will take to clean up the mess. For obvious reasons it's not a priority at this time. A backdrop to this destruction is the lush green tropics, still beautiful despite everything.

When we entered port a ship pilot was taken aboard. The pilot slowly guided the ship to the mooring birth (out anchorage) where the ship dropped anchor in forty feet of water about a half mile off shore. With this done we were immediately given eight hours shore leave. All hands prepared to go ashore. The uniform of the day was dress whites. As I was going ashore in the launch I was immediately splashed with salt water and diesel oil. Blast!! My white uniform was covered with black oil spots. I didn't particularly want to go ashore looking the way I did, but I had no choice.

I went ashore with a signalman named Maurice Syat. I like him. He has a great sense of humor. Under different circumstances he'd be a good comedian. First, we roamed about Honolulu. The city was no longer the popular tourist spot it had once been. There were no ukuleles, flower lays, or hula dancers. Maury kept voicing his disappointment at the lack of such things. Eventually we found ourselves on Waikiki Beach. It was very quiet. Instead of sun bathers we saw anti-invasion barriers on the beach, huge concrete piles driven deep into the sand and draped with steel netting. There on the beach I noticed this enormous banyan tree. It's believed to be a thousand years old. Just imagine! A thousand years old!! I can't even fathom it. I made a vow right then and there. I will return to this place someday and find that tree again.

Wednesday, December 8, 1943

After three days shore leave grew old. Many of us chose to stay aboard and entertain ourselves by whatever means were available. As it is, we're required to report back to the ship at sunset because there are not enough accommodations for so many men. Only submarine personnel can enjoy the full amenities of the plush hotel *The Royal Hawaiian*. They deserve it. Sub duty is probably the most dangerous and stressful job there is.

Thursday, December 9, 1943

Being on active duty is different than boot camp or service school. The petty disciplines for any small infraction of the rules are a thing of the past. I suppose it was part of the training, but it seems so ridiculous now. The rigors of boot camp, all those laps around the grinder and the commando course, have come to an end. We do, however, have ship board calisthenics every morning for about thirty minutes, but it's not too bad.

Friday, December 10, 1943
Movie night! Every Friday night while in port they show the latest movies. They are shown in the "fan tail" (the stern of the ship). In order to hear the sound the blowers are turned off. The blowers provide ventilation below deck. While they are off it's sweltering and impossible to go below. Of course, everyone is watching the movie and there is no need to go below. Tonight's movie was "Casablanca", with Ingrid Bergman and Humphrey Bogart. Great movie!!

Saturday, December 11, 1943
Today Bill Anderson came back from shore leave showing off a new tattoo. Apparently he gets a new tattoo in every port. He has an obsession with tattoos. I see more of his "art work" than I care to see in the shower. There's no modesty among 1400 men confined in a comparatively small area. I've seen quite a variety of tattoo artists' work, but Anderson's is the most extensive. In addition to having his ship the North Hampton on his chest, he has two ship screws (propellers) tattooed on each buttock with the words "twin screws, keep clear" above them. On each leg he has a nude woman from hip to foot. The rear view is on the left leg, the front view is on the right. He has something tattooed in the instep of each foot, but I don't have enough interest to find out what it is. On one arm he has "For God and Country"

and on the other he has "Mother". I'll bet his mother is so proud.

Friday, December 17, 1943

Our time in port is just about up. The Boston has been assigned to a task group in the third fleet with Admiral "Bull" Halsey as the O.T.C. (officer in tactical command). I've also learned that the third and fifth fleets are one and the same. The only difference is who's in command. Admiral Halsey is in command of the third fleet and Admiral Raymond Spruance commands the fifth fleet. Both are four star admirals. The designation is merely a change of command. The amazing thing is the Japanese are unaware of the ruse. They actually believe there are two different fleets. Incredible!! I should also mention there's also a seventh fleet, but it's smaller and made up of older ships.

Monday, December 20, 1943

We are underway. I'm a little seasick. I think I can probably expect to be seasick every time we leave port. I carry on. It's better if I don't dwell on it.

I understand we are headed for the Gilbert Islands to take part in that offensive. These are a chain of Japanese held islands on the equator. Within the group we have two large essex class (full size) carriers, two cruisers besides the Boston, and sixteen destroyers.

There is a lot of speculation about what we will run into. I am quite excited about what the future will hold.

Tuesday, December 21, 1943

An amusing incident happened this morning. Well, amusing in regards to one person, unfortunate for another.

Our ship, needless to say, also serves as a troop ship. We transport marines for active duty. One marine, in particular, was having a terrible time with seasickness. At breakfast his sergeant, a loud stocky man, was admonishing him. "What are you a Marine or a pansy? A soldier can always eat. You have to eat. SO EAT!!" he yelled as the Marine shoveled in the food. All of a sudden the Marine, unable to keep it down, explodes all over the table right in front of the sergeant. The sergeant bolts up from the table. From his gut he makes a sound like, "aaaccchhh oh man". He quickly exited, looking extremely gray. How quickly the tables turn.

Wednesday, December 22, 1943
While leaving San Francisco I thought the activity on the bridge was pandemonium, but it was nothing compared to what it is now. There are many more tasks to be done when operating as a part of a group, such as: reading and recording the flashing light, flag hoist, spying the command ship with the long glass, and keeping the log. I am totally confused these first days at sea. I seem to have forgotten all that I learned in service school. I'm having trouble remembering the alphabet flags and their order. I'm having the most difficulty reading the flashing light. Morse code is a language all its own.

Chief Zook is riding me all the time. I think he thinks I'm too lax or not dedicated enough. At times he can be amicable and friendly toward me, but that ends if I do something contrary to his thinking. He has an annoying habit. When he wants to tell me something, he signals me using semaphore signals. He is very sloppy at it and I can never understand what he's trying to tell me. This isn't our usual means of communication. He only uses this when he wants to irritate me.

Saturday, December 25, 1943

Christmas Day! I've never spent Christmas away from Chicago. This tropical climate, plus being in the middle of the ocean adds little to the holiday spirit. As Maury Syat said, "I don't know why, but it just doesn't feel like Christmas this year." Our Christmas celebration was meager. We had services on the main deck followed by a turkey dinner. I should mention we have services every Sunday as well. Our chaplain's name is Spitzer.

Monday, December 27, 1943

The Gilbert Island operation is well underway. Of course I witness none of it being miles from the action. I watch each day as flight operations are conducted from the aircraft carriers. Bomber and fighter escorts take off four times a day and proceed to the Gilbert Island target where they bomb the Japanese fortifications. All this is in preparation for the eventual marine land assault. I don't envy the marines in having to do this. I'm thankful to be aboard ship and for not having to take part in any such landings.

Planes returning after dark transmit a secret identification signal called an I.F.F. (identification friend or foe). They use red, blue, and green lights, flashed intermittently in varying order. For example, red, blue, green, or green, blue, red, or red, red, blue, and so on. These signals change every half hour. An incorrect signal will result in an aircraft being fired upon.

Wednesday, January 5, 1944

Recently, a few of the guys on board have been trying to get a band together. They found out I play the saxophone and asked me to join them. We managed to borrow some instruments from the ship's band and had a "jam session". We sound lousy.

The ship's band, on the other hand, is really good. They play every evening one hour before sunset on the ship's well deck. The well deck is a wide open area between the forward and after superstructures on the main deck. They play the latest music of Tommy Dorsey, Glenn Miller, and Benny Goodman, just to name a few. I love this time of day; relaxing up on the deck, watching the sunset, and listening to great music. At the end of the concert they play taps, the flag is lowered, and the ship is made ready for black-out.

When my watch follows the concert the mood carries over. All is quiet and serene. We talk about home, family, and girls. The "old timers" tell of the great liberties they've had in their time. Because I'm from Chicago everyone thinks I'm a gangster. I deny this of course, but because most everyone is from the east coast and know very little about Chicago, they insist on my telling them stories about the "mob". I tell them these stories are merely hearsay, and then continue to tell them about the St. Valentine's Day massacre of 1929 and other such infamous incidents. I'm surprised at how intently they listen, although I do tend to stretch the truth a bit. They all gather around. I feel like a story teller. I believe they actually look forward to the next time when they can hear about Al Capone and the sinful era of prohibition. By nature I'm more of a quiet type. So this attention is quite a departure for me. I rather enjoy it. So what if I tend to color things a bit? No one is the wiser.

Being aboard ship out in the middle of the ocean, we all do our small part to help pass the time. Another person who has a knack for entertaining everyone on the bridge is Anton Auresciccio. He is a signalman striker like me. He sings this song that goes on for ever. It must have a thousand verses. It starts out like this: "The other night when I came home as drunk as I could be, I saw a...". From there it goes on and on and on. Auresciccio is a short, heavy Italian. We refer to him as Mr. 5 by 5, picture Mr. 5 by 5 up on the balls of his feet, rocking from side to side, singing this goofy song. It's pretty funny.

Friday, January 7, 1944

We have fish every Friday night. The fish are frozen and have been in the hold since the ship was commissioned. I don't like fish, so I usually skip supper on Friday nights. The navy beans we have are not bad at all. We have beans three times a week, for breakfast on Monday, for lunch on Thursday, and supper on Saturday. They are plain, white beans which have been boiled. Then we douse them with catsup. The only meat served is spam and dried beef. The beef is served with gravy on toast, commonly called S.O.S.. The beans are my favorite. It's a good thing since we eat them three times a week. The food may be just all right, but the cakes and pies are incredible. I've never tasted any better. It's generally agreed upon that navy "bakers" are the best in the world.

Here's a distinguishing note: it is called supper for the ship's crew, but for the officers it's called dinner. I suppose there must always be a distinction between officers and the enlisted men, but the navy could never operate with just officers. The enlisted men are the backbone of the U.S. Navy.

Wednesday, January 12, 1944

The Gilbert Islands have been secured with minimal casualties. The results of this offensive show just how much strength the armed forces are starting to build up.

The fleet is returning to an advance base called Tarawa atoll in the Gilbert Islands. An atoll is an extinct volcano, which is surrounded by a coral reef with a lagoon in the center. Apparently the entire fleet will be contained in this lagoon. I can't even begin to picture this.

Thursday, January 13, 1944

This atoll is really something to see. As I said an atoll is an extinct volcano. The rim projects above the surface of the water. There are palm trees, lush green vegetation, and white sandy beaches. Under different circumstances this would be an island paradise. There is an opening in the rim just large enough for a ship to pass. Within is the lagoon, which is actually the crater of the volcano. The lagoon is about one mile across and there are about 75 to 100 ships here. These are not all naval vessels, but also non-combat ships like oil tankers, repair, and supply ships. After all is secured the opening is closed with a steel anti-submarine net. This prevents enemy subs from entering. The net will be removed when the fleet gets underway again.

Friday, January 14, 9144

Movie night! Now that we are in port again we have movies on Friday night. This perks everyone up. Tonight we saw "Johnny Come Lately", with Jimmy Cagney.

Saturday, January 15, 1944

Mail from home!! This is even better than movie night. However, I did receive some bad news from my mother. My grandfather, Henry Leary, died. He was 94 years old. I saw him last just before entering the navy. My mother and I made the trip to Seymor, Iowa to visit him. I always got a kick out of him. He carried an old railroad pocket watch which he wore on a long chain. He would watch the time and every hour or so he'd say, "Time for my walk, Tommy". If we were sitting on the porch, he would get up shuffle to the other end and back, than take his seat again. Sometimes he would be up for a longer walk. We might walk to the street corner and back. After the walk he'd take out his watch, shake his head and say, "It took me forty-five minutes today." I was sorry to hear he had passed away.

When I joined the navy I was told I needed a middle name. Since I had never been given a middle name, I took my grandfather's name and became Thomas Henry Miller.

Monday, January 17, 1944

While moored in this Pacific atoll we are allowed to go ashore each day. However, we still stand our watches, four hour on, eight hours off. While ashore we have warm beer parties and pretty much just horse around. Today Maury Syat posted a sign that said "Naugatuck, Connecticut 9,137 miles" with an arrow pointing east. Naugatuck is his home town. He's a character.

Tuesday, January 18, 1944

I went swimming today and got the scare of my life. As I mentioned before I'm not a great swimmer. I was floating not too far from the reef when I saw a big dorsal fin about twenty feet away. SHARK! I panicked and started to thrash around in attempt to get back to shore. In doing so I cut my foot on some coral and it began to bleed. This was not good! I know that sharks are attracted to blood, but the shark seemed to remain motionless. Maybe my thrashing scared him. Fortunately, I wasn't the only one to see the shark. At that point I heard a gun and the shark was riddled by rifle fire. Marine sharp shooters were patrolling the area in motor launches just in case such a situation should arise. All in all, I guess I was never really in any danger. The shark was then hauled up on shore and completely dissected. Its teeth were taken out and passed around as souvenirs. The eyes will be dried and polished then made into a key chain or an ornament. I didn't get any of these mementos. I think I should have though, because I'm sure I saw him first. All I have to show for this adventure is a nasty cut on my foot.

Wednesday, January 19, 1944
My first tropical island experience was quite exciting, but it is now growing monotonous. It rains every hour while the sun shines brightly. Rainbows are commonplace around here. After it rains it is very hot and humid.

Thursday, January 20, 1944
While the ship is at anchor all hands "turn to" cleaning and painting. Using wire brushes the old paint and rust are scraped off. Everything is then repainted in drab battleship gray. There are no brass fittings that might reflect the light. All this is to ensure that the Japanese are unable to spot us. All deck hands called deck apes, seaman, and non-petty officers must "lay themselves to the task". Aside from sweeping and mopping the deck after a rain, I have been

exempt from this task, primarily because I have my watches to keep.

Friday, January 21, 1944

The ship is being refueled. We'll be heading out again shortly. We are also taking on supplies. We are getting fresh fruit and eggs from the States. This will be a real treat for a few days while the supply lasts. Then it is back to our regular sea rations.

The movie for tonight was "For Whom the Bell Tolls", starring Gary Cooper.

Saturday, January 22, 1944

Today is my 25th birthday, but it was like any ordinary day. I never mentioned it, so no one knew about it.

Monday, January 24, 1944

We will be underway again shortly as apart of the same task force under "Bull" Halsey. As part of the bridge personnel I'm in a position to get first hand information. From the information I've obtained the war department has implemented a bypass strategy. In this plan we bypass the Japanese held islands and invade the intermediate islands. These intermediate islands are secured and used as advance bases. We then move on to secure the next. Blockades are set up so no supplies can reach the Japanese held islands. The Japanese soldiers on these islands are destined to starve or become completely disarmed. However, this is no easy task. The soldiers on these islands are very resourceful and can live for years without supplies.

There are many Japanese held islands. They extend from the Japanese mainland down into the South Pacific.

They are the Gilbert Islands, the Marshall Islands, the Marianas Islands, the Caroline Islands, New Guinea, the Solomon Islands, Truk Islands, Wake Island, and Okinawa. These are just a few. Of course some of these islands have already been secured, but it is more than obvious the end of this is a long way off.

We will be on our way to the Marshall Islands. The scuttlebutt is this operation may last two to three months. The rest of the ship's crew is pretty much in the dark as to where we are headed. When ever I go below to the compartment everyone pumps me for information. There's a lot of talk and speculation and it makes me feel good to know they consider me a reliable source.

Tuesday, January 25, 1944

We got underway early this morning, just after sunrise. Again, I felt a little seasick, but it passed after a few hours. There are three aircraft carriers, two heavy cruisers, three light cruisers, four battleships, and twenty destroyers. I can't name all the destroyers. I'll never be able to keep track of all those little babies. The carriers are the Enterprise, the Yorktown, and the Saratoga. The Yorktown is one of the new full-sized essex class carriers built just before the war began.

It's an awesome sight to see the silhouettes of these carriers against the horizon, especially the Saratoga. This monstrous ship started out as a battleship and was converted to an aircraft carrier in the 30s. She has a distinctive outline against the horizon. The Japs know her outline too. The carriers are always their main target, but they would especially love to sink the "Sara". What a line "Tokyo Rose" would have to broadcast if such a thing happened.

42

Monday, January 31, 1944

The Marshall Island offensive continues. Aircraft take off and land four or five times a day to make their bombing raids. Nothing much else is happening. Our routine consists of daily calisthenics, signal drills for those not on watch, fire control and abandon ship drills. Sometimes we're required to air our bedding if the idea comes to the upper echelon. It sounds like a good idea, but in the process of airing the mattresses they also become soaked from the ocean spray.

The activity on the bridge seems less hectic to me. Perhaps I'm getting more accustom to it. These days my duties include raising flag hoist and assisting those who are reading the light. Reading and recording the flashing light is a tricky business. The rate of receiving is about six words a minute. Just a blink of the eye can cause you to miss something. I try to read and operate the light, but I get messed up. Someone usually has to help me out or take over. My problem when reading the light is that I try to anticipate what each word will be and this is a big mistake. When you think a certain word will be transmitted and something else forms, it's very confusing. I have to try and keep my mind blank and wait until the coded characters are complete before forming any words.

Saturday, February 5, 1944

I've been fortunate lately to be standing watch with an old chief signalman instead of Chief Zook. Chief Williams is a fatherly old man who was called out of retirement. He is very tolerant and patient. He does not harass me. Because of him I am becoming more confident and can operate efficiently. I'm on my way to becoming a full-fledged signalman (I hope).

Tuesday, February 15, 1944

An incident occurred tonight on my watch that really startled me. There was almost a head on collision with an aircraft carrier. This was the result of misinterpretation of "night signals". This signal was sent during the day, to be executed at night on delay. There was an error read into the course change. This could have resulted in a catastrophe, but fortunately they were able to maneuver the ship so as to avoid a collision.

During this incident Lt. Schwartz, who was in charge, was ranting and raving and carrying on; reasonably so I guess, but he was just a bit too dramatic and not helping the situation at all. He was pacing back and forth and shouting, "This negligence will cost us the war," and in the same breath, "WHERE'S MY COFFEE!"

This was an unusual occurrence. Normally our watches at night are so quiet. It's a challenge at times to maintain our watchful vigil. Looking out to sea at night one sees many strange illusions. The phosphorescent white caps, caused by algae stirred up by the ship's propeller, sometimes give the impression of torpedo wakes.

Monday, February 28, 1944

This operation has been going on about a month. Other than the aircraft that take off and land there isn't much else to report. All and all, things are quite dull for those of us left behind. I keep hoping to see some Jap planes coming in for attack, but they are always intercepted by our carrier fighters and never reach the group. There are constant warnings of "bogeys" (unidentified aircraft). In this situation we all report to general quarters and maintain our battle stations. My battle station is on the forward part of the signal bridge doing nothing except standing with a pair of binoculars. So far these warnings have amounted to nothing. The old timers tell me, "When you least expect it something will happen".

Wednesday, March 1, 1944

The routine has passed from dull to down right boring. We continue on a zigzag course. There are many courses and they change constantly. The most common plan is "zebra". It's the most confusing for anyone who might be trying to determine our course.

Little by little I'm getting the hang of things around here. I can operate most of the time on my own. I've become pretty close with about half of the signal crew, or the "gang" as they are referred to. However, I'm still having a problem with Chief Zook. I can't figure him out. Sometimes he's genial toward me and other times he's cruel. I don't know if I admire or respect this man. I do know I don't deserve some of the treatment I've received from him.

Saturday, March 4, 1944

We were running low on supplies and fuel oil. We had to refuel several destroyers from our own fuel supply. These smaller ships are not able to stay out as long because of their limited fuel capacity. This morning we rendezvoused with oil tankers and merchant marine supply ships with… mail from home!! This amazes me, the fact that we can meet in the middle of the ocean unbeknownst to anyone. I mean, the location of the U.S. Fleet is top secret. The folks back home have no idea what's going on out here, except for what is given in radio broadcasts and newspaper, all of which are very vague. It's also quite clear how important our supply lines are. Success depends on them. After all this is what we are trying to do to the Japs, cut off their supply lines.

I previously mentioned Bill Jackson, quarter master third class. He received a letter from his wife today. I came upon him while he was reading it and there was no avoiding him. I was stuck hearing the whole letter. He always wants to read his wife's letters to me, telling me how much she loves him and all that. Today's letter really caused me to wonder about him. It seems his wife asked him if she could date the man next door. "It's purely platonic," she said. He said he trusted her completely and didn't think it was fair to ask her to sit at home and pine for him. I can't believe it. Is he dense or what? I responded, "yeah, I guess." Then I tactfully said I didn't think he should read me his mail. I hope that will put an end to it.

Thursday, March 9, 1944

I survived the "Neptune Ceremonies". We crossed the equator today at 1200 hours, more or less. What followed was mass mayhem!! The "scull and cross bones" flag was hoisted during the ceremony. I wonder if the Japanese could somehow see this, what would they think. *Are they at war with themselves?* The ordeal was brutal. Some wound up in sick bay with broken bones.

The ceremony stems from the legend of Davy Jones, King Neptune's emissary and royal scribe. Davy Jones must initiate all "pollywogs" that dare cross the line (the equator) into the domain of Neptunis Rex. If found worthy they become one of his trusty "shell-backs" and are accorded all the rights and privileges within his domain: "The Solemn Mysteries of the Ancient Order of the Deep."

The ordeal lasted from sunrise to sunset. Those already initiated stood watch and manned the ship. I wonder what would have happened if we had been attacked by enemy aircraft. I'm sure this was planned and carried out with the certainty that there would be no interruption from the Japanese.

About five hundred of the ship's company were initiated in the ceremony. All were required to strip down to their shorts. We were drenched in salt water and diesel oil. Then we had to run a gauntlet of men armed with electrified pitch forks and cloth clubs filled with wet sand. The deck became wet and slimy. As we ran it was impossible to keep from falling. Then we were shocked and beaten. We struggled to get up and then continued running to a huge tank filled with salt water, diesel oil, and slop (garbage) the consistency of mud. There was no way out except to enter the tank and make your way to the other side and climb out. All the while being beaten and shocked. Next, we passed through a slimy tunnel and crawled to the other end through the same offensive stuff (about two hundred feet). Last of all, we were sprayed with a black sticky stuff and covered with fine ground up kapok and mattress filling, sort of like being tarred and feathered. The ship's chaplain was excused from the ceremonies, but he elected to participate and endure it with the rest of the men. A noble gesture I think.

The ceremony took all day because of the clean up afterwards, which was no small job. I think I may have broken a rib. Plus, I have many bruises and the back of my neck is very sore from a blow I took. I'm glad it's over and I'll never have to go through it again.

The Journal of T.H. Miller

Monday, March 20, 1944
The Marshall Islands offensive is taking months. Great resistance is being met in the bypass procedure by enemy aircraft fire, but our bombings are taking a toll and our aircraft losses are next to nil. The enemy fighters are no match for our new "Hellcat" fighters and "Avenger" bombers.

Thursday, March 23, 1944
We've anchored in another advance base. This atoll is on the secured Kwajalein Island in the Marshall Islands. We will be here about a week while the ship is being cleaned and painted. Even before we reached port, side cleaners are piped to standby to "turn to" side. Side cleaners are then lowered over the side to wire brush and paint the entire hull. The whole ship is cleaned and painted. They say a navy ship is the cleanest thing in the world. That may be true, because it is swept down three times a day and swabbed once a day.

Friday, March 24, 1944
I was told when you least expect it, expect an enemy attack. Well, what happened tonight proves this to be true.
It was movie night. The lights were on like a night time baseball game. We were watching the movie "Frenchman's Creek" with Joan Fontaine, when one lone Jap plane managed to sneak through our radar defense system. It's not even known where he came from. He dropped a bomb, but it landed in the water and didn't do any damage. We immediately blacked-out, went to general quarters, and maintained our battle stations, but it was too late. The enemy plane eluded us and the s.o.b. escaped! I regret that we were never able to see the end of the movie.

The Journal of T.H. Miller

Thursday, March 30, 1944
After one week of warm beer parties and doing very little else, we'll be heading out tomorrow. I'll be ready.

Friday, March 31, 1944
We put out to sea early this morning. On this operation there are two small aircraft carriers, the Princeton and the Belleau Wood. These are light carriers about half the size of the big essex class carriers. Also with us is the Ben Franklin, a big carrier and the command ship of the O.T.C. (officer in tactical command). Besides the Boston, there are two light cruisers the San Juan and the Vicksburg. In addition to these ships there are about twenty destroyers.

The activity on the bridge is as hectic as ever, but I'm use to it now. I'm doing much better reading the flashing light. Everyday I see improvement in my performance. Lately, I've been assigned the long glass. With a telescope my eye is constantly trained on the command ship. When a flag hoist is displayed by the command ship I immediately record and call out the command. In response our flag is raised to the "dip", which means halfway. When the signal is understood, the flag is "two-blocked", or raised completely to the top of the mast yard. This procedure is followed by every ship in the group. When every ship displays the signal in the "two-block" position, the originating ship will "haul down" (lower) its hoist and that "purport", or signal message will be executed. There is a competition between the ships in the group to be the first to "two-block" the signal. There is one destroyer who's maybe twenty miles from the command ship and he wins it every time. I don't know how he does it?

The Journal of T.H. Miller

Monday, April 3, 1944
We are still on the Marshall Island campaign. It will take months to secure and completely immobilize these islands. It's been uneventful so far. I haven't seen any other Japanese aircraft.

Again, our O.T.C. for this operation is "Bull" Halsey. I can see him through the long glass sitting in a chair by the bridge rail, wearing his baseball cap, and over-seeing the operations of his fleet. He epitomizes the wearing of a baseball cap, not because of the popularity of the game, but because such a notable person established the tradition. We have some fun with it. We all spot the O.T.C. to see what he's wearing. If he's wearing a baseball cap, we all wear our baseball caps.

Friday, April 7, 1944
Today I made a very serious mistake!! While on the long glass I was spotting the command ship. I read a flag hoist which displayed two flags, a "turn" pennant and a #9 numeral flag. A "turn" pennant designates a "flank" movement of ships, like marching men who all turn simultaneously. The numerical flag is employed many ways. In this case it means 90 degrees. The configuration, #9 flag above the turn pennant, means all ships turn 90 degrees left. A #9 flag below the turn pennant would mean all ships turn 90 degrees right. I read the signal as left turn flank movement, but recorded in the book incorrectly as a right turn flank movement. No one was aware of the mistake. When the signal was hauled down (executed) I was astounded, as was everyone else, to see all the ships passing by us in the opposite direction! I immediately realized what had happened. I called the navigation bridge over the

intercom to cancel the signal. "Be-lay that last signal!" I shouted. "We know! We know!" they answered.

It was a careless mistake which we had been cautioned and warned about in service school. The cardinal rule is: Do not memorize signals. Use the "Bible", the "International Signal Book". The incident caused quite a furor. It took half an hour to turn the ship around and get back into formation. I am fortunate nothing serious happened. It so happened that the ship's captain, Captain Larson, was taking a nap and the officer of the deck at the time was very tolerant, leaving the punishment up to the communication division. Now I'm really in for it! Chief Zook has been waiting for something like this to nail me on. I'll be swabbing decks and standing extra watches for the next month.

However, a new procedure was devised to preclude such an incident from happening again. Two men are now assigned to spot the command ship, one to record the tactical signal in the log and yet another to assure the accuracy and purport of the signal. It was jokingly said that the new procedure would be named after me. "Yeah," said Maury Syat, slapping me on the back, "you're a hero!"

Monday, April 10, 1944
Action continues in the Marshall Island. The Marines are meeting stiff resistance. I still haven't seen any enemy aircraft.

Thursday, April 13, 1944
It's very hot and humid here in the tropics. We're required to wear dungarees and long sleeve shirts. Only the top button is allowed to be opened. This is very

uncomfortable. There are many cases of prickly heat that progresses into open running sores. We've discovered that after shave lotion is a good cure.

Friday, April 14, 1944
Today we had our first taste of an air-raid. There had been constant reports of "bogeys". All morning we were at general quarters manning our battle stations. I'm still on the forward part of the signal bridge on the lookout with my binoculars. There was nothing to see, but I felt on edge. We were maintaining our course using a zigzag plan. I didn't see anything from the forward port side of the signal bridge. All of a sudden the anti-aircraft batteries cut loose. The ship started shaking. The noise was deafening. My ear drums felt like they would burst. The five inch anti-aircraft guns and the forty millimeter quadruple mounts were firing all at once. The sky filled with tracer trails. I still couldn't see anything. Then, suddenly I saw about eight planes flying abreast, low, just above the water, and coming toward us. I could see the tracer tracts going into those planes, but they kept right on coming toward us. Then one erupted into flames and then another. They hit the water with a huge splash. A great explosion followed as their torpedoes exploded. It was all over in a matter of seconds. A cheer went up from all hands celebrating the victory. I was, momentarily, elated, but the feeling was short lived, there being no real call for celebration. I can't help but think about the crew that perished. I'm only doing my job. I never hated the Japanese, or anyone for that matter. Despite the fact that they are the enemy, there are mothers and fathers and loved ones who will receive notice that some one has died. I regret this and

clearly see how senseless it all is. I hope against hope that it will end soon.

Thursday, April 20, 1944

I've been informed that the "flag" is supposed to have a third class signalman in its roster. Since such a rank is lacking, I am eligible to take the exam. I have an uneasy feeling certain people are going to take issue with this, namely Chief Zook. There's nothing he can do to block it since I am not part of the ship's company.

Thursday, April 27, 1944

I've made signalman third class. Lt. Nichols told me I made a high grade on the test. Needless to say I was accosted by Chief Zook and berated for not going through the proper channels for advancement. Proper channels, I suppose, would have been to go through him, so that the request could promptly be denied. I really don't care what he says. I'm rated now and have become quite proficient in operating despite the hazing I've received from him.

Monday, May 1, 1944

Today I was informed that the "flag" will be transferred to the cruiser Baltimore. When the Admiral transfers ship, as his staff, we go as well. The Baltimore is a sister ship to the Boston. They are identical in all aspects, so I expect things will not be too strange other than having new shipmates. I will miss most everyone in the "gang", but I'll be glad to be out from under Chief Zook.

Friday, May 5, 1944

I packed my gear and with the other flag personnel, Zimmerman and Jackson, reported aboard the Baltimore. The Boston, in the mean time, is headed back to the States. I wish I were on board and heading home too.

Payday! As third class signalman I get $60 a month.

Friday, May 12, 1944

I've been on the Baltimore for one week. The atmosphere is much different than it was aboard the Boston. I immediately felt a sense of camaraderie with the signal "gang". I don't know why. It's nothing like I felt coming aboard the Boston. The guys, Fred Keating, George Swiden, Constantino Aryanas (a Greek), and Patrick Sterpe, all seemed to take to me at once. They are all first, second, and third class signalmen. The Chief Signalman's name is Riley. I see very little of him on the bridge, only when he comes up for a cup of coffee. "Is the joe pot on?" he always asked. I marvel at what a change this all is from the Boston. I'm having the time of my life on the bridge.

This is a monstrous armada this time: carriers, battleships, cruisers, and many destroyers. We are still somewhere in the Marshall Islands. Nothing exciting is happening. I've seen no more enemy aircraft.

Monday, May 15, 1944

On the bridge I'm first man of the watch. This status is supposedly given to the most efficient man. I hold this position even though I'm only rated third class. I've been told I'll make second class soon as long as I've been given these duties. We'll see.

The Journal of T.H. Miller

Friday, May 19, 1944

We are heading into heavy weather. Each day the sea grows progressively rougher, the winds higher, and the waves bigger. We've tried to avoid it, but we're heading into a typhoon! It's difficult to steer away from the storm because its direction is impossible to predict. In this weather flag hoist is out of the question.

Saturday, May 20, 1944

It's been difficult to stay in formation. Orders are to scatter if it becomes too severe and severe it has become! We string lines across the open areas on the windward side because it is impossible to walk without danger of being blown overboard. The waves are mountainous. They seem to rise a hundred feet above the ship. The ship rolls heavily, rises to the crest of a huge wave, then plunges into the abyss at the bottom of the swell. The bow disappears; water rushes up and over the main batteries. This happens continuously.

Sunday, May 21, 1944

The heavy weather continues. Of course they couldn't hold church services on the well deck. We have services in the mess hall during inclement weather.

Monday, May 22, 1944

This storm has been going on for days. I believe it's even getting worse, if that is possible. We must remain on the bridge. We are unable to function in any way, but if you are on watch, you are on watch. If we go from port to starboard we must hang on to the lines.

One of the old timers was telling me about a guy who foolishly tried to judge the time between waves. He tried to run across the dangerous area of the well deck where the swells wash across. Just as he was half way across, he was caught by a huge wave and washed overboard. His body was never recovered.

At the end of my watch I went below to the compartment. To go below you must stay within the superstructure. I decided to be a dare devil. When I reach the main deck I opened the hatch and stepped out. This was the lee side of course (out of the wind). The area between the fore mast and the main mast is a wide open area. A tremendous wind was blowing through this area. I was smart enough not to venture beyond the hatch, but I stood there a few minutes and took in the awesome site. All of a sudden the ship seemed to tremble. A great wall of water crashed across the ship. That was enough for me! I went inside and made my way along the lower decks to the compartment. Here in my bunk it is impossible to sleep. The ship is pitching and rolling and staying in the bunk requires a firm grip. Some of the guys are praying and saying the rosary. I send up a prayer too. They say there are no atheists in a fox hole. I think it would be safe to say there are no atheists in a typhoon either.

Wednesday, May 24, 1944
We are finally out of the heavy weather. The ships are regrouping after being separated by hundreds of miles. The Japanese had their hands full too, if they were out at sea. You might say the war was postponed due to weather.

Thursday, May 25, 1944
Today we pulled into Eniwetok atoll. An advance base in the now secured Marshall Islands. We will be here

for several days, reconditioning the ship and taking on supplies. While here we anxiously await mail. Some of the guys receive perfumed envelopes with lipstick kisses and the letters S.W.A.K.. I guess this means "sealed with a kiss". I don't get any letters like these. It's just my family and friend who write to me. I did have a pen pal after boot camp, but that ended after a couple of letters. I never was much of a letter writer. I could never get romantically involved with anyone at this time. It would only complicate matters. I've seen and heard too many "Dear John" letters.

Friday, May 26, 1944

Movie night! Tonight we saw "The Seventh Cross" with Spencer Tracy. Get this, the movies are for the enlisted men. The officers are invited as our guests. Sometimes things digress from the original purpose. Proof of this is the officers get the best seats and the movie isn't started until the officers are seated. Tonight we waited fifty minutes for the movie to start because one of the officers was sleeping. When he finally showed up the entire crew clapped. He did not appreciate the applause.

Monday, May 29, 1944

Duty while anchored in these places is light. We stand our normal four hour watch, but the rest of the day is ours. We go ashore for warm beer parties when they can spare us, but these tropical islands are so hot and humid and it rains every couple of hours or so. I spend most of my off duty time reading. I've read a lot of books.

Thursday, May 31, 1944

We are underway again. It's the Marianas Islands this time. We have been re-designated the fifth fleet under Vice Admiral Marc Mitscher. The force consists of three essex class carriers, two battleships the West Virginia and the Iowa, the cruisers Baltimore, Houston, and Canberra, and twenty four destroyers. With so many destroyers I can't keep all their names straight. I can only identify them by their hull numbers.

Thursday, June 1, 1944

The sea is smooth as glass, a far cry from the raging ocean the last time out. We are headed into the doldrums around the equator. This is as awesome as the storms. The sea is without a ripple. The water is so clear. I can see thirty to forty feet down.

These latitudes were avoided in the old days of sailing ships because the ships would be "becalmed" for days. Sometimes the crew, using row boats, would have to tow the ship out of still water. I can't imagine trying to tow a great sailing ship by such a method.

There is quite an optical illusion. Looking at the other ships they appear motionless on the water. I'm reminded of the poem "The Ancient Mariner", by Samuel Taylor Coleridge:

The Journal of T.H. Miller

The Ancient Mariner

All in a hot and copper sky
The bloody sun, at noon
Right up above the mast did stand
No bigger than the moon

Day after day, day after day
We stuck, nor breath nor motion
As idle as a painted ship
Upon a painted sea

Water, water, everywhere
And all the boards did shrink;
Water, water, everywhere
Nor any drop to drink

Friday, June 2, 1944
This operation has been uneventful so far. Carrier operations continue with planes taking off and landing three or four times a day. Because the sea is so calm we have had to increase our speed to flank (maximum speed), which is 38 knots about 42 miles per hour (land speed), so that our planes have enough wind to take off.

We are in the "horse" latitudes. According to legend, Spanish sailing ships loaded with horses became "becalmed". All the horses died and were thrown overboard. They floated in the still waters for days. That must have been a gruesome sight.

Tuesday, June 13, 1944

The Marianas operation continues, with a focus on Saipan, Tinnian, and Guam. These are important bases, hard fought for and strongly defended by the Japanese.

Wednesday, June 14, 1944

It seems that the Japanese naval commanders have ordered their naval forces east of the Philippine Islands. There's talk that this may be the next naval offensive.

Thursday, June 15, 1944

The fifth fleet is now moving to intercept the Japanese naval forces in the Philippine Sea. We're all wondering if we will witness the action. We are going crazy on the bridge. There are constant warnings of enemy aircraft approaching.

Monday, June 19, 1944

Tonight our fliers were returning in the dark, almost out of gas. Mitscher ordered all ships to turn on their lights, despite submarine danger. A few planes, out of gas, ditched in the water, but all pilots were rescued.

Tuesday, June 20, 1944

This action in the Philippine Sea has turned out to be a great air battle. I have learned that the Japanese have lost over 300 planes and their crew, just in the last four days. We are pursuing the remnants of the Japanese fleet who are now retreating. In this pursuit we have sunk two small supply ships, the carrier Hiryo, and badly damaged the carriers Zuikaku and Chiyada. Despite all this activity, I've yet to see a single enemy aircraft. This is not unusual since task groups operate out of range from each other. One group may see action, while the other may not. I have to ask myself, why am I so anxious to see action? I should be grateful for my sideline seat at this event, and yet...I'd like to see something as long as I'm here.

Wednesday, June 21, 1944

Every ship has two observation planes. Their purpose is to spot the enemy, check on our firing accuracy, and conduct air-sea rescue. They are catapulted into flight and land on floats in the calm wake of the ship. Anyway, late this afternoon our plane came back after scouting the area. The pilot climbed out of the cockpit soaking wet. He looked utterly exasperated. "It's never like this in the movies," he said shaking his head. I wonder how he got all wet.

Friday, June 23, 1944

This has been a long operation. All the bigger ships must refuel the destroyers from their own fuel supplies. We are to rendezvous with oil tankers at dawn with mail from home.

Thursday, June 29, 1944

The scuttlebutt is that the invasion of the Philippines is set for sometime in December. It all depends upon the securing of the Marianas Islands; once secured the islands will serve as a supply and submarine base, then the invasion will begin. After our success nine days ago, they believe the islands should be secured within four to six weeks. We shall see. Anyway, here we are in the Philippine Sea aiding in these air-strikes.

Saturday, July 1, 1944

This afternoon there were warnings of "bogeys".
Since transferring to the Baltimore I haven't been assigned a
battle station. The bridge was very crowded, so I requested
permission to go below. The chief granted my request. I felt
safer, but I also felt a little cowardly. Shortly after, the order
was sent out that all hands third class and lower were to clear
the bridge. This made me feel better. We were down below
when all of a sudden the ship's anti-aircraft batteries let go.
The ship shuddered, trembled, and shook with all the guns
firing. Needless to say I didn't see any of it.

Monday, July 3, 1944

Surprise, surprise! I was assigned a new battle station
today. I now report to the after superstructure where I
operate a telephone, which I can't get to work. What's worse
is now I have no excuse to hide!!

Thursday, July 20, 1944

They're meeting little resistance in securing the
Marianas Islands, so we've been deployed to the Caroline
Islands for mop up work. These islands are to be so
completely destroyed that it will be impossible to function
even as a supply base. We're secured from general quarters,
but remain at condition two. This is an alert condition with
the possibility of enemy planes being detected on radar.

Sunday, July 23, 1944

I was on watch this morning at 4am. It was very quiet
and I was having a hard time staying awake. I must have
dosed off, because I dreamt I was a kid in a candy shop. I
could even smell maple. It turned out the cooks were

preparing pancakes for breakfast. What I smelled was the maple syrup. When I woke up it was disappointing to realize it was only a dream.

Tuesday, August 22, 1944

We are headed for Hollandia, New Guinea where the ship will go into floating dry dock. Apparently there are so many barnacles on the hull that it's slowing the ship down.

Wednesday, August 23, 1944

I'm amazed! Floating dry dock is an incredible thing to see. Just off shore this monstrous ship is sailed into a huge reservoir (the only word I can think of to describe it) and all the water is pumped out, but the procedure is not as simple as it sounds. As the water is pumped out divers go down and place blocks, which are manipulated by cranes, under strategic points of the hull. Then, balancing on hundreds of these wooden blocks, she sits high and dry in the huge empty tank that is as wide as two city blocks. Simply amazing!! It gives me a funny feeling to walk around beneath this ship. I can reach up and touch the keel.

Friday, August 25, 1944

Movie night! Tonight we watch "Since You Went Away" with Claudette Colbert. Tomorrow we're going ashore for a beer party and…entertainment!!!

Saturday, August 26, 1944

The entertainment was good. We've been starving for something different and this was a needed change of pace. There was a vaudeville show with Ray Milland. I was disappointed in his performance. He was really out of character. He thought he had to be raunchy and I just didn't care for it. Bob Crosby and his band played for us. Now, that I did enjoy. There were no girls of course, so the guys were all dancing with each other.

Thursday, September 7, 1944
We are out at sea again. We shipped out during the early hours on the fifth. We have joined the third fleet. Our group consists of two big carriers and two small light carriers, five cruisers: the Baltimore, the Quincy, the Vicksburg, the Houston, and the Canberra, and the usual destroyer screen.

Friday, September 15, 1944
Not much is happening. The usual false alarms, waiting and watching, but nothing ever happens. The air strikes, three or four times a day, are softening things up for the Philippine invasion I guess. The usual launch and recover of our aircraft returning from sorties (strikes). The usual acts of preparedness as they're called: routine, drills, ect.

Monday, September 25, 1944
I am not happy. The flag is being transferred again, this time to the light cruiser Vicksburg. I've become really close to these guys and I don't want to leave. Only three of us are leaving at this time, a yeoman, the admiral's steward, and me. I'm thinking, *why me*? They tell me they must have a signalman as one of the first personnel. I guess the rest of the staff will come aboard later.

Tuesday, September 26, 1944
The mid-ocean transfer did not go without a glitch. First of all, there was a mistake in the assignment. I was not

to board the Vicksburg but the light cruiser Houston. I was informed of this at the last minute. Not that it matters. What does matter is they never expected me on board the Houston. What confusion! I haven't been assigned a watch or anything. This is miserable! I wish I could go back to the Baltimore and say, "I'm back. They didn't need me," but that's not possible.

Saturday, September 30, 1944

I've been aboard the Houston for four days now. I'm in a state of confusion regarding my duties. I have no specific watch, so I operate on my own assuming the usual four hours on eight hours off. I was told by the second class signalman and "Master of Arms", whose name is Tietelbaum, "Just show up for muster every morning at 0800 hours, so you will be recorded in the log book." That's it. Tietelbaum is kind of a wise guy. He frequently makes stupid remarks like, "Chicago was never like this, eh?"

Monday, October 2, 1944

A young kid, seaman first class, has latched on to me. He can't be over seventeen years old. His name is Jimmy Alteiri. When I'm operating the signal light, he jumps at the chance to record for me. I feel sorry for him. He's so young. He should be home shooting marbles, not being shot at. I find myself looking out for him.

Friday, October 6, 1944

It seems enemy aircraft are headed our way. They are operating out of air bases on Formosa. However, all Jap airplanes are intercepted by our fighters before they even come close to the group.

Thursday, October 12, 1944

Today started out and progressed like any other day, but the ending was a different story. It was sunset and we were at general quarters. There had been continuous radar warnings all day. Our fighter planes had all come back. The sun had set. Dusk is very brief out here and darkness comes quickly. I'm standing at the port rail of the bridge and couldn't believe what I saw. There was a line of about twenty low flying aircraft. All of a sudden they were all around us. At the same time every gun on every ship was firing. The ship was shaking and vibrating. I saw flashes followed by explosions as those planes, one by one, crashed into the water. One was headed toward us in flames. He was bent on crashing into our ship, but he fell short about fifty feet from our port side. I could feel the heat from the explosion. That was just a little too close for me! As suddenly as it started, everything was quiet again. There was a lot of excitement as we evaluated the damage. It wasn't long before we realized that the Canberra had been torpedoed! I could just barely see her in the darkness. She had stopped dead in the water. There was no order to abandon ship, so I guess damage control was doing their job.

Friday, October 13, 1944

We continue underway with the group, but three destroyers and one light aircraft carrier are deployed to stay with the Canberra and defend her against further attack, which is certain to happen, while she is being towed back to port for repairs. Naval intelligence must have anticipated something in this operation, because sea going tug boats were also assigned to sail with the group in this offensive.

Today is just like any other day, boring. The incident of last night seems to have been forgotten. The air strikes continue every two hours. The enemy planes never make it past our fighters. It's apparent the U.S. Navy pilots are better trained. The Japanese Mitsubishi planes, on the other hand, are not inferior to ours. They are completely void of armor plate. This makes them more maneuverable, but they also fall apart under pressure.

Last night's attack has generated some real concern. These guys are coming out after sunset. We have <u>NO</u> night fighters! That's why they were able to hit the Canberra. Reports are we are destroying their airfields on Formosa. I suppose this is the reason for this new tactic.

Saturday, October 14, 1944
So much has happened in the last twenty-four hours, I don't know where to begin relating it. My story begins at sunset on Friday the thirteenth. Yes, Friday the thirteenth. We were at general quarters. It was about a half hour before sunset. I had a strange apprehension. The sea was not rough, but there were many white caps. It was getting dark. I was standing on the ladder (a steel staircase) on the outside of the superstructure that leads to the bridge. Having no particular station, I paused at the landing looking out to sea (starboard side). About a mile away a thunder storm was moving toward us. It's amazing to see a rain storm approaching while at sea. Low and behold, out of this cloud bank I saw about fifteen aircraft emerge. Japs! Flying low off the water. At that point all hell breaks loose. Our guns erupt at once, as did the guns of every ship in the group. The fire power of the guns is deafening. It feels like the vibrations will jar the feelings in my teeth. I was transfixed as I watched these

planes hit the water and explode. The sky was full of tracer trail. These were torpedo planes. The Japanese torpedoes are superior to ours. They are powerful, accurate, and deadly. Plus, they rarely miss. Suddenly the ship shudders under me. My first thought was we hit a reef. The ship rose up and then rolled steep to port then starboard. I felt and heard an explosion that came from below the deck. A huge radar antenna from up on the main mast came crashing down, it hung there by the guy and mooring wires that had supported it. It was at this point that I realized what had happened. We'd been hit! Torpedoed!!

I didn't know what to do. I felt myself start to panic. I said a short prayer and a calm feeling came over me. I didn't have a life jacket or anything. I went to the bridge. The word came over the intercom, which was activated by voice vibration after having lost all power: Abandon ship! The chief signalman, who I hadn't met until now, showed up and asked if I had been trained to operate the infra-red signal light. This light is used at night, but the receiver on the other end must be set up and ready to receive. I told him it wouldn't work if the ship recovering didn't have the unit activated. He insisted I give it a try. When I got no response he said, "To hell with it." That was the last I saw of him. Again, I began to panic, but I settled down after a quick prayer. I went down to the main deck. The rail was even with the water. I told myself I would never complain about being bored again. Just then Jimmy Altiere came up to me in a state of panic. He was almost in tears. I told him to put on his life jacket and wait. About that same time some guys asked me to help them release a life net and get it into the water. I gladly helped them. They took Jimmy into the net, but when they asked me to get in I refused. I wasn't about to go over the edge. That was the last I saw of Jimmy, but I'm sure he's safe. It was pitch black by then. I'm not sure, but I think there was a moon. All of a sudden search lights from all the other ships began sweeping the ocean looking for survivors. I heard about three hundred guys went over the side either in life boats or life jackets. Suddenly, there was a great deal of commotion. Apparently the order to abandon ship had been rescinded. Now I'm really glad I didn't go over the side

I spent the remainder of the night on the deck. It was slanting so that sleep was impossible. Of course I dare not go below. It was still hard to realize what had happened. Like a dream, I kept expecting to wake up and find out it never took place. I'm not sure how, but eventually the night passed. Finally, day light came. I saw all the other ships underway. A tug boat had arrived to take us in tow. A small carrier and three destroyers were also deployed to accompany us. The rest of the task force continues on the operation. Meanwhile, the admiral's barge was sent to pick up the three men of the flag. How about that! It seems Rear Admiral Wiltse was very concerned about his three men. I'm now back on board the Boston.

The Japanese lost about forty aircraft in exchange for disabling two cruisers in two days. I'm not sure how to measure victory, but this doesn't seem like much of a gain to me.

Sunday, October 15, 1944
Being back on board the Boston is not so bad now. I'm considered a survivor. Chief Zook has been made Ensign, so he has nothing to do with me. Zook's an ambitious man. Very few are promoted to commissioned officer from an enlisted rank. I admire him for his

determination. I too have been promoted to second class signalman. So in my own way I'm coming up too, I guess.

Monday, October 16, 1944

Today the twenty four men that perished in the fire rooms of the Canberra and Houston were buried at sea. Their bodies were brought aboard the Boston yesterday. It was the most moving ceremony I'd ever seen. All of us looked on wearing our dress white uniforms. The ship's band played The Navy Hymn, "Eternal Father". While the band played the words went through my head:

Eternal Father, strong to save, whose arm has bound the
Restless wave, who bade the mighty ocean deep
Its own appointed limits keep. Oh, hear us when
We cry to thee for those in peril on the sea.

Then, wrapped in canvas shrouds, the chaplain blessed each body before lowing it into the sea. There are no white crosses to mark the graves of these men, for those who die on the deep, lie in the deep.

Tuesday, October 17, 1944

Today before departing the Admiral decided to go aboard the Houston to assess the damage. I was assigned to go along in the Admiral's barge to do visual signals if necessary. While the old man was looking things over I remained on the barge with two others. We had been waiting about an hour. The swells were tremendous. They swallowed us up. Everything in sight disappeared as we sunk. Then as we reached the top of the swell everything came into view again. I began to feel seasick. As a distraction, I'd been watching a giant shark swimming around the boat. He had made several passes, occasionally brushing the bottom of the boat. I could see the white of his belly as he came from beneath us. Impulsively, I did a very foolish thing. I took out my knife and plunged it into him. The shark bolted so quickly and with such force that there wasn't time to let go of the knife. I was jerked out of the boat. It happened so fast. Before I knew it the coxswain was pulling me back into the boat. I lost my knife. Somewhere in the Pacific Ocean there's a shark with my knife in his belly. Later the coxswain, whose name is Tom Delcastle, presented me with his knife to commemorate the occasion.

Wednesday, October 18, 1944
The Japanese are determined in their efforts as they continue to pursue the already damaged Canberra and Houston. Despite the efforts of our fighters the Japanese did manage to make one more hit on the Houston. The second torpedo that hit caused the ship to come back on an even keel. She is no longer listing to the port side, but has sunk down so that the main deck is level with the water. It's a strange site to see nothing but the superstructure above the water. Now, as I write this, we are far removed from these damaged ships. They are well on their way to Pearl Harbor or some other advance base for repairs.

Friday, October 20, 1944
We have been assisting in the liberation of the Philippines. The invasion will probably be some time in December.
The Japanese have been sending out aircraft only in the daylight hours. I can't understand this. Do they lack

military strategy, discontinuing night air raids even after they have proven to be so successful? I don't know. Maybe they think their heavy loss of aircraft is not worth two of our cruisers.

Sunday, October 22, 1944

The air strikes continue. Again, the routine has become uneventful. All enemy planes are intercepted and destroyed. I'm not complaining, you understand. Since the events of the last month or so, I have no objection to routine and safe duty.

Monday, October 23, 1944

We are headed to Leyte Gulf where a series of overlapping sea- air battles are taking place.

Wednesday, October 25, 1944

The events of the last two days have been...complex. From what I understand the Japanese split their fleet into three different forces. A small force made up of empty aircraft carriers was used as a decoy to lure Halsey and Third Fleet away from Leyte Gulf and the Seventh Fleet. Meanwhile, the Japanese sent forces from the north and south in attempt to trap the now unprotected Seventh Fleet. Initially we were designated to back up Halsey and the Third Fleet, but apparently the ruse must have been discovered, because we proceeded to aid the Seventh Fleet instead. When we arrived there was a turn of events. The Japanese ships were caught between our two forces. The Seventh Fleet, under Admiral Clifton Sprague, which was out numbered by the Japs, attacked under cover of a rain squall. A brilliant move in my opinion, because somehow this bold action persuaded the Japs to believe that we had the upper hand, which probably wasn't the case. I don't completely understand it, but as far as I'm able to determine the Japanese are in retreat. All in all, it was a close fight. The Japanese forces which attacked from different directions and outnumbered our forces have been defeated. It shows the tenacity of the U.S. soldiers and sailors. Despite the odds the U.S. sent the Japs running. This battle for Leyte Gulf cost the Japanese twenty-six ships, four of which were carriers. The Americans lost only six ships, only one of which was a light carrier.

During this confrontation the Japanese have introduced a new weapon, the kamikaze. They set out from Formosa on their one way suicide trip. This is really awful! These planes do not always sink a ship, but they kill a lot of guys and do a lot of damage. They hit right on the bridge where I am. We haven't seen any of these kamikaze pilots yet and I hope we never do.

Thursday, October 26, 1944

Sometime during the last two days the carrier Princeton (a light aircraft carrier) was hit by a kamikaze plane. It was burning badly. We were on one side of her, while another cruiser was on the other side. We were trying to control the fire by spraying salt water onto it from our hoses. This is dangerous work. If the fire should spread to the ammunition or the fuel supply the result would be disastrous. Anyway, I was standing at the starboard rail of the bridge, taking all this in. I could feel the heat from the Princeton's hull as the fires rage below. On board there was just a skeleton crew for damage control. They are all dressed in flash gear, but I don't know how they could stand the heat.

All of a sudden we received an urgent order to cut loose at once and get as far away as possible. We did so immediately. Traveling at flank speed (top speed) we were about a half mile away from the ship when a great explosion occurred. I felt a shock wave of intense heat, but the funny thing is I never heard a thing. I'm sure the explosion must have been deafening, but I just don't remember it. I was transfixed. I couldn't take my eyes from it. I'm lucky, because thus occupied I didn't see a piece of metal coming right at me. It hit the bulkhead just two feet from my head. I truly must have a guardian angel. Meanwhile, in what seemed to be only minutes, the Princeton slowly started to roll over. After about twenty minutes, with her keel side up, she gradually sank and disappeared beneath the water. On the bridge men were sobbing after witnessing such a tragedy. All damage control crew are lost.

This war is beginning to break me down. It is hard to remain optimistic. At times I doubt my own survival and that scares me!

Friday, October 27, 1944

As a tired and battle weary force we head toward Hollandia, New Guinea. We'll be here only long enough to take on provisions, re-arm, and refuel.

Saturday, October 28, 1944

Mail from home, unfortunately it brings bad news too. I learned in a letter from my mom that two of my friends died during the invasion of France on June 6th, John Ronan and Henry Cox. I went to Henry's going away party when I was home on leave after boot camp. He was all army. At times we debated the merits of the army vs. the merits of the navy. His closing remark was usually, "The only reason you joined the navy is because the army wouldn't have you." It was all meant in fun and when we parted we sincerely wished each other well.

I knew of the invasion. We do get bits and pieces of what's going on outside in the world, but the idea of another war going on at the same time as this one is incomprehensible. Being so occupied with what's at hand, one simply can not spend much time thinking about anything else. Knowing we have a job to do, as do they, we carry on hopefully bringing the end a little closer.

Sunday, October 29, 1944

We are pulling out tomorrow. I understand we'll be proceeding as part of the Third Fleet under Admiral Halsey. We will be assisting in mop up efforts following the Leyte Gulf campaign. After that we are to proceed further north and assist in air strikes on Luzon, the largest island in the Philippines.

Tuesday, October 31, 1944

We crossed the equator again today. There were about two hundred "pollywogs" aboard the Boston. So naturally the "Neptune Ceremony" must take place. I took no part in them because I think the whole ritual is ridiculous. Instead, I offered to stand watch.

In addition to crossing the equator, we've crossed the International Date Line many times while on our different operations. This makes me wonder. If we keep crossing it and lose a day each time, does this mean we will never grow old?

Sunday, November 5, 1944
I'm making big bucks now! As a second class signalman I now make $72.00 a month. That's a lot of money considering there's not much to spend it on out here.

Saturday, November 11, 1944
Nothing much has been happening. It seems we suddenly find ourselves in the midst of action and then we go for weeks without seeing anything. I guess it's all to be expected.

Thanksgiving Day, November 23, 1944
For Thanksgiving we had our traditional turkey dinner with powdered mash potatoes. It was a welcome change from our regular fare of white beans, chip beef, and fish. Before dinner we had church services on the "well deck". Truthfully, I'm a little hard pressed to come up with anything I'm really thankful for. Except one...I'm still alive.

Saturday, November 26, 1944
We've been eating turkey soup, left over from our Thanksgiving dinner. They serve it with hard rolls, which we soak in the broth. It's good.

Monday, December 4, 1944
Everything remains quiet. There's nothing new to report.

Monday, December 25, 1944
Christmas Day! The Navy must be big on tradition, because this year's Christmas celebration was identical to last year: services on the well deck followed by another

turkey dinner, warm tropical breezes, and lots of water. What I wouldn't do to be home for Christmas.

Monday, January 1, 1945

All is quiet. We pass into the New Year without any celebration. It's just another day. I'm hoping to see an end to the war by this time next year, but the powers that be keep saying the end is nowhere in sight. We're not even to think about going home before 1950. Five more years! This is unbearable.

Wednesday, January 10, 1944

We have been at sea for over two months. It seems like I have been at sea my whole life. To me the earth is nothing but water. From the time I wake in the morning until I hit the sack at night, the first and the last thing I see is the ocean, the great Pacific Ocean.

These long operations are mentally stressful. Being together all the time you get on each others nerves. You eat, sleep, and work together. There is no escape. Arguments break out at times over petty insignificant matters. For instance, last night the 2400-0400 watch came on to find an empty coffee pot, which is unforgivable. Tempers flared and words were said which resulted in the 2000-2400 supervisor of the watch being placed on report for insubordination (who, by the way, was out ranked).

Being placed on report can lead to a "Captains Mast" all the way up to a General Court Martial. The "Captain's Mast" originated during the old shipping days when the captain held court at the main mast of the old sailing ships. It is the least of the trials and its penalties are not as severe as a court martial where the offender can be dishonorably discharged. At any rate, it's imperative to stay off report. As a rule, I never say too much, which is hard to do at times.

On a more serious note, I heard about this guy who went completely berserk. He climbed to the top of the main mast and wouldn't come down. Three corpsmen tried to subdue him, but he was so violent they had to sedate him and lower him down with ropes. I don't know if this is true; it's only what I heard. It shows what being at sea for a long time can do.

Tuesday, January 16, 1945

Air strikes are being launched on the Island of Mindoro in the Philippines. This is a small island south of Luzon. Today I got my first taste of a kamikaze attack. I saw four of these crazy guys coming in at us, all from different directions. One plane was flying low, level with the water; the other three were diving in at us from about four or five thousand feet. Tracer trails from our 40 mm quadruple mounted guns on the main deck obliterate the sky. Our five inch anti-aircraft guns are no good to us in this instance because they are unable to come into range on close targets. Two kamikazes nearly hit the carrier Ticonderoga. One hit one of our destroyers and another just missed our fan-tail. These guys are crazy!!

Friday, January 19, 1945

We've been under kamikaze attack for the past three days. We have not been hit, but there have been some near misses. Unlike the other enemy airplanes, our fighters are unable to intercept all of these suicide loonies. Somehow they've managed to get past them. I think they must have figured out a way to elude us while our planes are taking off and landing.

I've learned that the Seventh Fleet, which is operating in the Lingayen Gulf supporting the landing operations, is in a nightmare fighting off swarms of these kamikaze guys. Seventeen supply ships have been sunk and a total of fifty ships have been damaged.

Sunday, January 21, 1945

We are running low on fuel. As usual, we've had to refuel some of the smaller destroyers from our own fuel reserves. Today we were along side the destroyer Badger refueling her from our own tanks. It was very quiet, when suddenly we were alerted to "bogeys" on the radar screen. There was only a pause of anticipation before these guys were overhead, about fifteen suiciders intent on crashing into our ships. At this point it is impossible to fire upon them, because our fighters are up there and we don't want to risk hitting our own planes. The kamikazes were coming straight at us in point dives. When they were low enough and away from our aircraft we opened fire on them.

We immediately cut loose from the Badger. Both of us separated at flank speed. At about one hundred yards away the Badger was hit in the stern (fan tail). That Jap must have gone all the way down to the keel because she lost her steering mechanism and was going in circles. Another carrier had also been hit in this attack. Great billows of smoke were coming from the area of her bridge. It's such a helpless feeling to be standing on the bridge watching this, knowing nothing could have prevented it and nothing can be done to stop it.

Everything happens so suddenly. A sudden radar warning, suddenly they're over head and diving toward us, and then…it's suddenly over. The entire episode lasted only minutes. It makes my head spin and leaves me feeling sick afterwards.

Monday, January 22, 1945
I was on the 2000-2400 watch, entering the date in the log, when I realized that today is my birthday. It almost slipped by. Today I turned 26. God willing, I'll have many birthdays to come.

Tuesday, January 30, 1945
After exactly three months we are finally heading into port. We're going to Hollandia, New Guinea. I understand there may be some kind of entertainment when we get there. I heard it might be Bob Hope!!

Wednesday, January 31, 1945
Well, Bob Hope was too much to hope for, but there to entertain us was a black troupe. I hadn't heard of them, but they were good!! They had a great band that played the kind of music I love. There was a female trio singing songs by the Andrew Sisters. They sang "Beer Barrel Polka", "Tippy Tin", and "Boogie Woogie Bugle Boy". They weren't bad. They did a good job imitating the Andrew Sisters' sound. There were three tap dancers, who were supposed to be like the Nicholas Brothers. They were really good!! All in all, it was a pretty good show. Out here you appreciate anything you get.

The Journal of T.H. Miller

Thursday, February 1, 1945

Today I went ashore with a few of the guys for a warm beer party on the beach. While we were there someone discovered a large bone at the edge of the water. Some of the flesh was still on it and the smell was awful. A medical corpsman was immediately called. After examining it, it was determined to be human. About two months ago an ammunition ship blew up in the harbor, an apparent act of sabotage. When the ship blew up hundreds of crew members were aboard. From time to time their remains still wash ashore.

The smell was unbelievable. I know it's probably just my imagination, but it seems I can still smell it. Consequently, I've lost my appetite. I wasn't able to eat for the rest of the day.

Friday, February 2, 1945

While in port we are still required to stand watch. Four hours on, eight hours off. While here in Hollandia everyone wants to be assigned to the long glass. The reason is there's a naval hospital inland and those assigned to the long glass can watch the nurses, discreetly of course.

Being in port we get to watch movies again on Friday nights. It's been a long time since we've been able to do this. Tonight they showed, "A Place of One's Own" with James Mason.

Saturday, February 3, 1945

Tonight there was a dance on the main deck. The nurses from the hospital were invited aboard. The ship's band was playing and lanterns were strung overhead. It was quite sensational. Unfortunately, we weren't invited. "Sorry, officers only," we were told. About nine of us were watching all this from the signal bridge. Pretty soon one of the guys started in on Maury Syat, daring him to go down and ask one of those nurses to dance. Soon all of us were egging him on. Now, Maury will do just about anything, so we weren't too surprised when he actually did it. What surprised us was that he got several dances in before being escorted away. He'll have to pay for it though, by standing extra watches, swabbing the decks, peeling potatoes, or some such thing. I'm sure he'll consider it a small price to pay.

Tuesday, February 6, 1945
We'll be heading out tomorrow. I've enjoyed this time in port. I hate to think about going back out to sea.

Wednesday, February 7, 1945
We are headed to Iwo Jima. This island is located halfway between the Marianas Islands and Japan. The shelling has been going on there since August. I understand the invasion will be any day now.

Friday, February 16, 1945
We have been engaged in day and night continuous air strikes and ship bombardments. This has been going on for over a week. We stand off shore about five miles and lob shells from our main batteries, eight inch guns as they are referred to. The battleships Missouri and West Virginia are firing their sixteen inch main batteries. This is a coordinated effort. Between aerial strikes, the ships bombard the island. It is a shambles! The entire island is ablaze and clouded in smoke. I can't believe anyone is still alive.

The Journal of T.H. Miller

Monday, February 19, 1945
The marines landed on Iwo Jima today and were met by stiff resistance. Who would have thought anyone was still alive on that island? Apparently the Japanese pierced the volcanic rock with miles of hidden tunnels, thus making our bombardment efforts completely useless.

It may seem like a lot of trouble to go to for eight square miles of barren land, but let there be no mistake about it, this small bit of land is important to the Japanese. They use it as a radar warning station, a base for fighter interception, and emergency landings. For all these reasons, this small dot in the great Pacific Ocean is important to us too.

Wednesday, February 21, 1945
We have used up all the ammunition for our main battery. We must withdraw and rendezvous with tankers and ammunition ships to refuel and replenish our ammunition stores.

Thursday, February 22, 1945
An unusual incident occurred yesterday morning. Our task force was sailing westward from Iwo Jima. It was a clear, bright sunny day and all was still and quiet. I had been assigned to the long glass. All of a sudden the flag ship, the carrier Yorktown, sent up a flag hoist which was comprised of four flags: the "emergency" flag (a pennant) over three alphabet flags, "x-ray", "take", and "zebra". These flags are X, T, and Z respectfully. This is an emergency signal which purports the detection of an unidentified under sea vessel (a sub) that has been picked up on the sonar equipment. The location appears to be right in the center of our group. I ask

83

myself, is some fool Jap trying to make a suicide attack on us? Then three rocket flares shot up from the ocean. These are colored flares. Top secret identification signals. They burn brightly, undimmed even in the bright sun. Then a periscope appears. A U. S. submarine was surfacing right in the center of our group!

It looked black, slick, and slimy. At first all I could see was the conning tower with the white numbers 273. Then its bow was visible. She seemed to level out and was only about 500 yards from our ship. This was really something! Subs are literally "lone wolves". No one knows anything about them. Someone emerged from the hatch and was calling our ship. Our call sign, which is on our hull, #70 was being flashed by the sub. I immediately jump to the wing of the bridge to man the signal lamp. I call for a recorder. The message was short and brief:

> Relay to officer in tactical command:
> request permission to sail with group while
> repairs are made to damaged depth charge.

After the message was relayed to the flag ship, an all ships flag hoist followed: to submarine #273, "trigger", which means welcome.

The submarine sailed with our group for two days and one night until repairs were complete. Then almost as suddenly as she had appeared she began to submerge. All hands watched while she disappeared below the surface and was gone. I wish you well submarine #273 and Godspeed.

The Journal of T.H. Miller

Wednesday, February 28, 1945
We are headed for the East China Sea to assist on strikes on Formosa and also assist with air strikes on the Japanese homeland.

There are a lot of rumors about an invasion sometime in '45, but these are strictly rumors. It's my opinion that an invasion of the Japanese homeland at any time would be costly. No matter what happens, the Japanese are prepared to die for their country. They believe it is dishonorable to surrender and would rather give their own life in return.

Wednesday, March 7, 1945
We are running into rough weather. For three days we've been facing steadily increasing winds. I hope it's not a typhoon. I dread those things. Given a choice I'd rather deal with the Kamikazes than a typhoon. I believe everyone else would share in that opinion too.

Friday, March 9, 1945
We have received orders to drift apart. There is no sense in trying to stay in formation. We may as well let the storm have full sway. I feel a sense of false security when with the group. The security is gone now that we are separated by hundreds of miles, left all alone in this storm. I know being together won't protect us, but it goes back to the old saying "misery loves company", and being out here alone is miserable.

Saturday, March 10, 1945
We're in the middle of it now, mountainous waves and ferocious winds. This could go on for days.

Wednesday, March 14, 1945

The storm has diminished. It will take a day or two for the task force, which has been so vastly dispersed, to regroup. We just received word that the cruiser Nashville has lost about 100 feet of her bow, sheared right off by the massive force of the storm. Miraculously, the Nashville is still able to navigate. In spite of the damage done, her engines and turbines are still functioning. As usual there are several sea going tug boats sailing with us. Somehow they were able to locate her bow and have taken it in tow.

Friday, March 16, 1945

The group has come together again. The Nashville is with us. It's almost funny to see this great ship sailing without her bow. It looks like a half ship. I can see the steal bulk heads and the water tight doors all dogged down and shut tight. Her detached bow is mostly underwater, but with enough buoyancy to stay afloat. Just the sharp edge of her keel is above water. How the tugs were able to secure a line and take her in tow is beyond me. I guess this is what they are trained to do.

It's funny, one foresees and anticipates such damage, but we expect it to be inflicted by the enemy not Mother Nature.

Monday, March 19, 1945

The war, which was temporarily delayed due to weather, has resumed. The operation continues. Strikes on Formosa are taking their toll on the Japs.

The Journal of T.H. Miller

Monday, March 26, 1945

We have sailed north almost past the Japanese homeland. I don't think they know we are so close. It is not so tropical here. It's nice to have cooler weather. The tropics are okay, but navy regulation won't allow us to go without shirts and our battle with prickly heat has been an on-going problem while in the tropics. Maybe now we'll be able to put away the after- shave bottles and get some relief from this menacing rash where you scratch yourself raw.

Sunday, April 1, 1945

I am thoroughly fed up with being at sea. I'm beginning to believe the earth is nothing but water. Each morning when I come top-side from below, I see nothing but water.

Sunday, April 8, 1945

Very little to report, strikes continue.

Friday, April 13, 1945

We received word that President Roosevelt has died and Vice- President Harry Truman has been sworn in as our new president.

Friday, April 20, 1945

The flag is being transferred to another ship, the Quincy. The Quincy is a sister ship to the Boston and the Baltimore. They are identical ships, but with different crews. The Baltimore is going back to the States and the Boston is going into floating dry-dock. We are headed back to Hollandia, New Guinea to make the transfer. We'll be there only six hours before heading out again.

Saturday, April 21, 1945

While in port I had the opportunity to see the Houston. She's been here in floating dry-dock ever since that Friday the thirteenth in October when she was torpedoed. There's a hole in her hull that is large enough for a Greyhound bus to pass through. I wonder if they'll be able to repair her. The thought of her being nothing more than scrape metal is unbearable.

Sunday, April 22, 1945

The flag is scheduled to go on leave. A thirty day leave back in the States!! The good old U.S.A.!! Leave begins when we set foot in San Francisco. How about that? But…there's a catch. Only half the flag personnel can go. In order to be fair we will draw straws to see who will go back to civilization and who must stay behind to cope with the kamikazes and torpedoes.

10 p.m.

I drew the short straw.

Monday, April 23, 1945

I desperately wanted to go back to the States. I would have liked going home for a month to enjoy some of the things I took for granted before, like…well, everything.

I really don't know what's happening back home. I know defense factories are working day and night to produce war materials. I also know that gas and food are rationed, which is sad because there's a lot of waste out here. Food that's not eaten is thrown overboard.

Likewise, people back home have no idea what's happening out here. They have no idea where the fleet is or what losses we have sustained. Everything is top secret.

Those lucky enough to go home on leave are not supposed to say too much, because as the slogan goes, "loose lips sink ships". I don't really believe that though. I think Japanese intelligence is pretty much aware of where we are and what's going on.

Tuesday, May 1, 1945

We're just outside Leyte Gulf, supporting the invasion of Mindanao in the Philippines. The invasion was initiated on April 17th. We are sending in night flyers to intercept whatever they send at us from their remaining bases on Mindanao. MacArthur, our illustrious general of the army, promised "I shall return", but I'm sure he won't set foot on any island that's not secured.

Wednesday, May 9, 1945

So far this operation has been uneventful. I'm not complaining. How could I complain after my experience with kamikazes, bombs, and torpedoes?

My relationship with the other men onboard the Quincy has been strained. They are courteous but distant. I have a feeling they think "flag" personnel are to be avoided. I don't know why.

The communication officer on board the Quincy is Commander George Dunker. He is truly a civilian at heart. I heard he was some big shot with General Motors before being called up. Whenever there are unidentified aircraft in the vicinity, he looks wild eyed and says, "Someone is going to get hurt today." To which I can only reply, "I certainly hope not, sir."

Wednesday, May 16, 1945

The monotony of this operation is exhausting. The day passes as we progress from one task to the next: eat, sleep, stand watch, practice drills, all of which are done mechanically and with little thought.

Friday, June 1, 1945

We have departed from the raids on the Philippines. The scuttlebutt is we may be headed for the South China Sea for assaults on Indochina and from there possibly to the Sea of Japan for close support of the attacks on the Japanese homeland.

Friday, June 8, 1945

We are presently underway to assist in clean up operations on Okinawa. The islands of Okinawa have been under attack since April 1st. It has been the longest and greatest amphibian operation of the war, as well as the bloodiest.

The Okinowians are crazy! They've been brainwashed by the Japs and believe all American marines have murdered their own families in order to become marines. They believe there's nobody more blood thirsty on the face of the earth than the U.S. Marines. Furthermore, the Okinowains will commit suicide rather than allow themselves to be captured.

Monday, June 11, 1945

A very strange thing happened today. For the last few days there were a bunch of reporters from the NY Times and the Chicago Tribune on board ship. Apparently, they were anticipating a big story. Aside from taking a few pictures and conducting a few interviews nothing much was happening. Suddenly, they were told to leave. I don't know why. We get bits and pieces of information, which is more than the rest of the ship's crew, and yet we are still so totally and completely in the dark about everything.

Saturday, June 16, 1945
We've been deployed to act as an anti-aircraft defense. So far we've met little resistance. I'm no expert, but it seems obvious to me that the Japs are struggling. They're sending out all they got to attack our big carriers, but our fighters intercept them all and it's costing them dearly. Their losses are great. I can't see how they can go on much longer.

Wednesday, June 20, 1945
I hesitate to record what I saw today. It's probably best forgotten, but I'll never forget. Through the long glass I was able to see the marines using their flame throwers to rout the Japs/Okinowains from their caves. They shot the flames into the caves and the Japs came running out on fire. What a horrible death! I watch all this from the signal bridge, like a bystander.

Thursday, June 21, 1945
We've been at sea for two months.

Friday, June 29, 1945
We've withdrawn from Okinawa and are headed south toward Australia. We will pass through the South China Sea, the Dutch East Indies, and then out onto the Indian Ocean.

This is somewhat of a quiet time and I welcome it. We are aware of Jap scouts, but they are not attempting anything. They fly undercover of darkness and fog. There is one plane in particular that our radar and sound gear are able to identify. It must be an old, antiquated machine because it is slow and underpowered. We have given him the name "Washing Machine Charlie". We caught a glimpse of him just once. I'm not sure if he saw us or not, but he gave us no trouble.

I'm hoping against hope that this is the beginning of the end as this portion of the Pacific theater is pretty well secured. Even so, they still insist that the end will not come before 1950. I don't know if I can stand another five years of this. I'm sick of this war and all I think about is home.

Wednesday, July 4, 1945

We have been sailing for days it seems, but finally the group is entering Joseph Bonaparte Gulf in Australia. We've been granted six hours shore leave in Darwin. Allowing us only six hours is irritating, but what can anyone do? We moored off shore and were than towed to an assigned birth. An Aussie pilot was brought aboard to bring the ship in. Presently, we are waiting for the barges that will take us ashore.

8 p.m.

For the short time spent in Darwin, I had an experience I will remember all my life. It was about noon when we went ashore. Darwin is a fairly large city, but of course there were not enough accommodations for so many servicemen. I went ashore with six shipmates, but we got separated. So I was by myself and feeling somewhat lonely amid the masses of servicemen that filled the streets. I boarded a street car and rode around aimlessly. I don't know why, but at one stop I decided to get off. I was just wandering around when I decided to stop at a snack bar that was operated by a church mission. I sat down and had a cup of coffee. I started to read a magazine, but began to doze off. It wasn't long before I sensed that someone was sitting next to me. I opened my eyes and saw a little girl. She smiled at me and I said, "Hi". She answered in a pleasant Aussie accent. Before I knew it we were in the middle of a conversation.

She introduced herself. She told me her name was Christy and that she was ten years old. She said, "My parents told me if I ever saw a serviceman who looked sad or lonely, I should try to cheer him up." Then she asked, "Would you like to come home with me for dinner?"

I couldn't help but laugh. She was so blunt yet sincere. I said, "I'm neither sad nor lonely and I only have six hours, so I can't possibly come for dinner, but thanks for the invitation."

I thought this would end it, but she continued, "What are you going to do?" she asked.

"I don't know," I said. "I just might sit here. Or maybe I'll walk around until I find something interesting, something good that I'll always remember, something I can tell my friends about."

I was only making small talk, but she suddenly got very excited. "I know just the place!" she said. "It's a beautiful place on the ocean not far from here. We can walk. I've seen many pretty things there, rainbows, sunsets..." she hesitated, "once I saw the beautiful Blessed Mother."

Mmm, I thought, this kid has some imagination. "All right," I said. "I'd like to see this place."

The place she took me to was a small cove, with a sandy beach, and a cliff of rocky crags. There was a continuous ocean spray that produced a rainbow that seemed close enough to touch. It was indeed a beautiful place. I followed her as she nimbly descended to a lower cliff. There we stood about thirty feet above the water.

"My cousin and I dive into the water from this cliff, to catch coins that travelers toss into the water," she said.

"That's quite a feat," I replied.

"I could dive for you," she suggested.

I looked to the bottom of the cliff. I'm guessing the water was about thirty feet deep, but it gradually became shallow as it reached the beach. "No," I said. "You don't have to dive. I'll give you a half dollar."

"I'd like something from you," she explained. "Something like your dog tag that I can hold in my hand while I pray for you at night."

How could I refuse? The way I look at it, I'll take all the prayers I can get. So I took my chain and dog tags from around my neck and said she could have one. Then she suddenly tossed them over the cliff. She immediately kicked off her shoes and dove in after my tags. She disappeared into the water for about thirty seconds. Then she reappeared, popping up out of the water, with the dog tags and chain entwined around her hand and wrist. She put them around her neck and swam effortlessly to the beach. I made my way down the cliff, in a more conventional way. When I reached the shore she was just coming out of the water, laughing and dripping wet in her clothes, all shinny like a little porpoise. She looked like such a happy little girl. I gave her a hug and told her to keep my dog tags.

She saw me off as I boarded the streetcar that would take me back to where the ship was moored. She smiled and waved as the streetcar moved away. I watched her until she was out of sight. It was a wonderful afternoon and I can't think of any better company to share it with.

When I told my shipmates about what had happened, they made inappropriate remarks. Typical. I should have known they would be inclined to degrade my time spent with this exceptional little girl. She was uplifting and so happy. Just being with her lifted my sagging spirit. I'm not a religious man, but suddenly I began to wonder if she wasn't some kind of an angel. Is it possible that angels are walking among us?

Thursday, July 5, 1945

A funny situation came up yesterday afternoon as I was returning from leave. Well, it's funny now, but at the time it was quite startling. When I reached the pier I was alarmed to find the ship was gone. About twenty other of the ship's crew were milling about trying to decide what to do next when a large police vehicle pulled up and explained that the ship had simply been moved. We all piled into the paddy wagon and were transported to the ship's new birth about a half mile away. All the way the officials made jokes about us being A.W.O.L..

I've also learned the real reason for leaving the campaign and coming to Australia. I assumed it was to refuel and replenish supplies, but it was actually a different matter. Apparently one of our pharmacist mates has been accused of selling morphine and other opiates. I saw him as he was leaving the bridge. He was being escorted by armed guards to the barge that will transport him to the battleship Missouri where the general court martial is being held. He's been stripped of his stripes and naval markings. I can't help but feel sorry for him in spite of what he has done. I didn't know him, but I'd seen him around. He seemed quiet and friendly. He had four hash marks, sixteen years of service. What a shame to ruin a career because of lust and greed. It was poor judgment, pure and simple, but I haven't always exercised good judgment myself. I guess this is why I feel sorry for him.

With this business taken care of we head out again. From what I understand we are headed north to the East China Sea. This is a move, I'm sure, that the Japanese do not expect.

Saturday, July 14, 1945

We've been at sea for a little over a week as part of the fifth fleet under Vice Admiral Marc Mitscher. We are in the East China Sea between Japan and China, which is occupied by the Japanese. Our mission is to send air strikes against the Japanese homeland. This is risky business. Our planes are required to make extended flights. They are meeting resistance from enemy fighters out of Kyushu, Japan, but these efforts are ineffective in stopping our planes.

Wednesday, July 18, 1945

Air strikes continue. Our planes have been bombing everything they see in the harbor. It seems we may have over extended ourselves on this, because there is very little left there that would be considered a military target.

B29 bombers have been pounding the Japanese homeland since January of this year. I hear they are raining bombs and incendiary devises day and night. If the harbor is in this kind of shape, Tokyo must be a shambles.

Logically, the talk that follows is that the invasion of Japan is imminent. I know this will be costly. I've heard estimations of over one million casualties. One million!! How can that be justified? I'm sick of this war and I want to go home.

Thursday, July 19, 1945

The weather out here is cooler which is a welcome change. They say the water is less briny. This is why we don't have water hours. I don't know if this is true. I mean salt water is salt water, but it is nice to be able to take a shower any time of the day.

Thursday, July 26, 1945

There's been a lot of scuttlebutt going on lately about ending this war. We heard the Allies have issued the "Potsdam Declaration", demanding the unconditional surrender of Japan. To this I say, "What a great idea!!" I'm all for anything that will end this war!!

Tuesday, July 31, 1945

At this time the British Fleet has come into the Pacific to help us out. To be in accord with protocol we invite the "limeys" to come aboard for dinner. They took the invitation very seriously and conducted themselves in a sedate and dignified manor. They wore their formal dress uniforms, while we wore our usual uniform of the day, dungarees.

Ahead of me in the "chow line" was one of the British sailors. He was spirited and boisterous. All along the line he had loudly exclaimed over and praised the food. The drink of the day was cocoa. "What's this stuff, mate?" he asked the mess cook, with a limey accent. After learning it was cocoa he exploded, "Cow-cow!! Not even the bloomin King drinks cow-cow!" His response was hilarious. Everyone within ear shot roared with laughter, his laughter ringing out above all others.

Wednesday, August 1, 1945

This evening "all hands" were invited for chow on the British ship. Unfortunately, I was unable to attend because I was standing watch. I would have liked to have gone. I learned from those who did attend, the British sailors have tea time or "grog" time twice a day. The "grog" is equivalent to a shot of whiskey. They have the option of skipping "grog" time, yet they can still accumulate their unused portions. I wonder how they prevent someone from becoming sauced before his watch.

Saturday, August 4, 1945

Today we received classified information regarding the cruiser Indianapolis. From what I can gather, she was torpedoed by a Jap sub while on a secret mission. She sunk in about twelve minutes after radio distress signals were sent. An estimated eight hundred men are lost, but the survivors endured far worse, spending four days in shark invested water before being spotted by a surveillance plane. The Indianapolis had just left the island of Tinian, in Guam on the 30th. She was alone and unescorted!! This really must have been a secret mission.

The Journal of T.H. Miller

Friday, August 10, 1945
Japan has rejected our demand for surrender and has ignored the vague threat of "prompt and utter destruction".
10 p.m.
Our communication officer, Commander Dunker, came up on the bridge to talk to us as a group. The sun had just set, taps had been played, and the flags lowered. We were ready to head off to our designated areas when he requested we stay back. We were told that two bombs had been dropped. One on Hiroshima on August 6th, the other on Nagasaki on August 9th. The two cities are now nothing but rubble. 80,000 people gone, reduced to… nothing. It's unbelievable!! He said a new secret weapon had been used. He called it an "atom smasher" or some such thing. He also stated, with a hint of sarcasm, that on August 8th our "wonderful" new ally, Russia, declared war on Japan.

Tuesday, August 15, 1945
Japan surrenders!! The war is over!! Hostilities have ended. Unofficially, but be that as it may, the celebrating commenced. It was not a full scale celebration that one would expect for such an occasion, after all we are still out at sea. It's more of a jubilant atmosphere. The announcement was piped over the intercom. There followed a brief moment of silence as the information sank in. The realization came over everyone at the same time. There arose from everyone aboard a cry or a shout, an exclamation of some sort, as they grabbed the person next to them, hugging and dancing. As for me, I was so overcome I had to sit down right there on the deck of the bridge, from that vantage point I watched the others celebrating. I still can't believe it's over!

The Journal of T.H. Miller

Saturday, September 1, 1945
We have been anchored in Tokyo Bay for days. The harbor is full of ships. We have to be careful we don't run into any mines.

Sunday, September 2, 1945
Today the Japanese signed the surrender document. The actual ceremony took place on the deck of the battleship Missouri. I tried to observe it through the long glass and was able to make out some of what was going on.

Monday, September 3, 1945
We are going ashore tomorrow. Leave in Tokyo! A month ago I wouldn't have thought it possible.

Tuesday, September 4, 1945
The war has left Tokyo a sad a depressing place. The city is a shambles with no buildings standing. The streets are clear, but on each side are piles of rubble. There is no transportation. Streetcar rails are in place, but there is no power, or cars for that matter. The people are destitute. They are trying to sell anything and everything, even their daughters, for chocolate and cigarettes.

An old man stopped me and, in what English he could speak, sold me this small teak wood pagoda (a family heirloom?) for a carton of cigarettes and a Hershey bar. Unfortunately, I lost it before I even got back to the ship. I must have set it down and accidentally forgotten it. It's probably been resold. Ah, such are my fortunes of war.

The Journal of T.H. Miller

Monday, September 17, 1945
I've since been transferred to the cruiser Vicksburg. We are on our way back to Hawaii. This is a pleasure cruise with movies every night and no more blackouts. All lights are burning brightly.

I've been enticed to join the Naval Reserves as a way of getting discharged on points. I'm way over the requirement. I am now on reserve! As soon as we hit the States I will be separated from the "regular navy" then honorably discharged. I'm required to serve four years with the reserves, which means I could be recalled in the event of an emergency. I don't think that will happen, at least I hope not.

Saturday, September 22, 1945
We reached Pearl Harbor and moored in the destroyer-cruiser base. Now the only thing to do is wait patiently (ha) until it's time to go home.

Monday, October 1, 1945
I'm back on board the Baltimore and on my way home!! It's about a five day cruise to the mainland. The lights are on and the battleship paint has been stripped from the brass fittings. Everything is polished to a shine. Now, this is peace time navy!

I'm having a great time with my old buddies from the Baltimore, whom I haven't seen since being transferred from the ship. I feel closer to these guys than anyone else in the navy.

Friday, October 5, 1945

We arrived in San Diego to a rousing welcome. There to greet us was Dale Evans and about 100,000 cheering people. There was music and everything. Along the shore there was a huge sign that said, "Welcome Home! Well Done!" I felt like a hero, but I know I'm not. We all lined the rail in our dress whites. The United States! I'm lost for words when I try to describe what I was feeling. After one year, ten months, and five days I'm finally home, back in the good old USA.

Our mustering out papers and orders have been finalized and provided in an amazingly short period of time. We're on leave for the rest of the weekend. On Monday morning I'll board a train en route to Chicago and Great Lakes N.T.S., where I'll be honorably discharged. Until that time my great shipmates from the Baltimore and I are going to do this town in style. With my separation pay, 1,410 dollars and…50 cents, burning a hole in my pocket all I can say is look out San Diego.

Monday, October 8, 1945

The past weekend is somewhat of a blur. I heard straight whiskey and water is great. I was told you can drink a lot without getting drunk or sick. WRONG!! We really did this town right, stopping at all the night clubs and bars along the Hollywood Walk of Fame. We visited the Hollywood Palladium and saw Lana Turner, but we couldn't get near her. Later on we met some nice girls and danced most of the night, they where really nice to us, with our battle ribbons and all. The girl I met claimed to be an actress. She could be, I guess. She was pretty enough and a good jitterbugger too. The whiskey caught up with me eventually, so we went back to our hotel near dawn. We were crazy enough to start out the next night and do it all over again. This time I met some marines and got separated from my friends. I woke up sometime the next morning behind a billboard. I had no idea where I was. I was already late getting back to the ship and, therefore, was considered AWOL. When I did get back to the ship the officer of the deck just said, "Get your gear and get on the bus, immediately." I never had the opportunity to say goodbye to my friends and I regret this.

So here I am on a train, somewhere in Utah, and headed for Chicago. I'm going home!

Friday, October 12, 1945
After a four day train ride I arrived at the Great Lakes Naval Training Station to be separated from the US Navy. After several hours of interviews, I was given various documents outlining my talents and qualifications for civilian life. Finally, I am honorably discharged.

I'm still in uniform, but I'm a civilian now and on my way home. As I write this I'm riding public transportation free, my last benefit provided by the government. I wonder what lies ahead for me. I see life from a new perspective, after facing this near death experience. As a result I have a more profound appreciation of freedom and the luxury of being able to come and go and do as I please, wherever and whenever I please. I'm ready to take up my life where I left off. I hope it's a long and full life.

Chronology of the naval career of T. H. Miller

The Gilbert Islands Campaign
November 1943

The Marshall Islands Campaign
January 1944

The Mariana Islands Campaign
June 1944

Battle of the Philippine Sea
June 19-20, 1944

Battle of Leyte Gulf
October 23-27, 1944

Iwo Jima
February 1945

Okinawa
Air strikes: April 1945

Potsdam Declaration issued
July 26, 1945

Hiroshima
August 6, 1945

Nagasaki
August 9, 1945

Japan surrenders
August 14, 1945

Surrender papers signed on the bridge of the battleship Missouri, anchored in Tokyo Bay
September 2, 1945

The Journal of T.H. Miller

Epilogue

After being honorably discharged from the navy Thomas Miller returned to Chicago. Trying to pick up where his life left off, he returned to his old job at W. H. Hutchinson and Company. He spent several months there making bottle caps before deciding to take advantage of the GI bill. He enrolled at the University of Illinois and attended classes at the Chicago campus on Navy Pier. After discovering his interest in civil engineering he completed his education at the Illinois Institute of Technology. In 1953 he started working for the State of Illinois as a civil engineer with the highway department. He retired in 1985 after thirty-two years of service.

He served his four years in the Naval Reserves. In 1949 he was called up to serve in Korea. It was an anxious time for him as he waited for his notice, but his time in the reserves was up before he had to serve.

In 1949 he was on a double date with one of his buddies. Apparently, he must have preferred his buddy's date to his own, because a couple of weeks later he was dating her instead. Her name was Arletta. She was a nurse working at Augustana Hospital, in Chicago. They were married in 1951 and celebrated their fiftieth wedding anniversary on September 1, 2001. They had six children. Their oldest son, Paul, influenced by his father also joined the navy and trained as a helicopter pilot. Sadly, in 1990 while training for Dessert Storm Paul's aircraft was lost in the Pacific Ocean off the coast of Oregon.

Tom's navy experiences had a pleasant influence on his family. Cocoa, within the family, was always referred to as "cow-cow". White boiled beans, "navy beans", were prepared from time to time. He would enthusiastically encourage everyone to try some, never having lost the taste for them. "Dowse them with catsup," he would say. "You've never tasted anything like it." Unfortunately no one ever acquired the taste for them. And there was the "navy blanket", cream colored and 100% wool, quite possibly the warmest blanket in the house. It was the extra blanket, because it could never be unfairly designated to one person.

Two notable occurrences took place some forty years after returning home from the Pacific. In 1982 Tom, with Arletta, traveled back to Japan. This journey was met with mixed emotions. However, all uneasiness was soon alleviated. He felt amicably welcome, which in all honesty he never expected. It was encouraging. Forty years, after all, is a relatively short time to forgive, forget, and move on. Finally, in 1987 Tom and Arletta went to Hawaii. He thought about that old banyan tree. There on Waikiki Beach he saw it again, still standing after forty-four years.

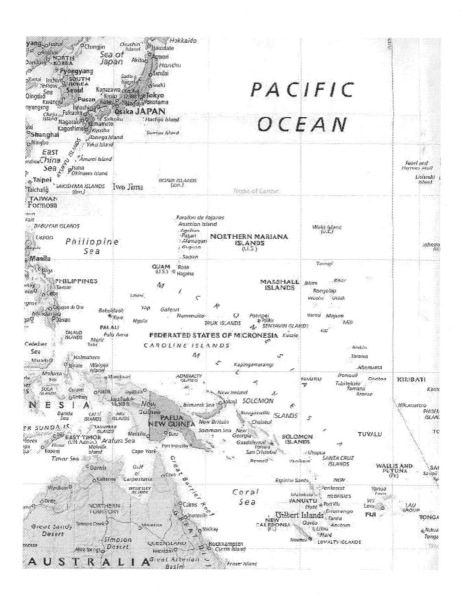